W9-AGS-128

# GOD KEEPS HIS PROMISE

A Bible Story Book for Young Children

GOD

# KEEPS HIS PROMISE

A Bible Story Book for
Young Children

Cornelia Lehn

Illustrated by Beatrice Darwin

Evangel Press
Nappanee, Indiana

Faith and Life Press
Newton, Kansas

Herald Press
Scottdale, Pennsylvania

Copyright © 1970 by Evangel Press, Nappanee, IN 46550; Faith and Life Press,
Newton, KS 67114; and Herald Press, Scottdale, PA 15683.
Second printing 1977.
Library of Congress Catalog Number: 76-90377
Printed in the U.S.A.
Designed by John Hiebert

# PREFACE

*God Keeps His Promise* is a Bible story book written to help the believing community share its faith and life with young children. The home and the congregation recite and celebrate God's great acts in history, and see God at work in the present. Humbly and reverently the community shares the Bible with children in its midst—acquainting them with the heritage of the church, sharing with them the world view of the people of God, and helping them perceive their worth and place in the community.

The stories in this Bible story book are planned to be read and told at home and in the Sunday school. They have been carefully selected and written so that, on one hand, they do not distort the story the Bible tells, nor, on the other hand, overlook the growth, development, and readiness of little children. Bible stories have a way of speaking for themselves and contributing to many learnings. No attempts have been made to add applications, or morals, or interpretations to these stories. However, confidence in the Word, in loving relationships, and in the presence of the Holy Spirit leads us to expect learnings and experiences in the lives of little children that could scarcely be planned or programmed.

Over four centuries ago (1541) Menno Simons wrote, "Therefore, let everyone take heed, if he truly loves his children, that he acquaint them rightly with the Word of the Lord as soon as they have ears to hear and hearts to understand; that he direct them in the way of truth, and zealously watch over all their doings, that they may from youth learn to know the Lord their God, fear, love, honor, thank, and serve Him."

Scottdale, Pennsylvania                   Paul M. Lederach, D. Ed.
June 1969

# CONTENTS

# THE FIRST HOME

Genesis 1:26; 2

Long ago God made the first man. He called him Adam.

God wanted Adam to take care of all the earth, but would Adam know how to do this?

God planted a beautiful garden in Eden. He made many different kinds of trees grow out of the ground.

Some were shady,
some had fruit on them,
some were lovely with flowers.

God made a river flow right through the garden to water it.

Then God took Adam into the garden.

"Adam," said God, "this is your home now. Take good care of it."

Adam worked in his beautiful garden home. He sowed seeds. He picked flowers. He trimmed trees.

God saw that Adam took good care of the garden, but God also saw that Adam was very lonely.

"It is not good that the man should be alone," said God. "I will make him a helper."

So God made many animals. He let them
run
and jump
and gallop
under the trees and by the water.

God made many birds.
They sang,
they called,
they whistled.

God watched to see what Adam would call them.

9

Adam looked at each animal and each bird to see what it was like and what it was for. Then he gave the hippo-pot-a-mus a name,
    and the squirrel,
      and the deer,
        and the tiny, tiny mouse.
Adam gave each bird a name --
    the roo-oo-ster,
      the duck,
        the robin, and the owl.
God saw that Adam took good care of the animals and the birds.

But Adam was still very lonely. There was no one with whom Adam could talk and laugh and sing. There was no one to help him take care of the garden and the animals. There was no one like Adam that could live with him.

So God made a woman and brought her to Adam to be his wife.

Now Adam had someone with whom he could talk. Now he had someone to help him. Now he had someone to live with him. Adam called his wife Eve.

Adam and Eve took good care of their garden home. God saw they would learn to take care of all the earth.

# ADAM AND EVE DISOBEY GOD

Genesis 2:15-17; 3

When God showed Adam his garden home, God said, "Adam, you may eat the fruit of all the trees except one." God showed Adam the tree. "If you eat fruit from this tree, you will die."

Adam understood. He knew which tree it was.

11

So Adam said to Eve, "See this tree? God said we must not eat the fruit of this tree. If we do, God said we will die."

Eve understood. She knew which tree it was.

But one day, the serpent said to Eve, "Did God say you should not eat fruit from any of the trees?"

"Oh, no," said Eve. "He said we may eat fruit from all the trees in the garden except one. We must not touch this tree. If we eat fruit from it, we will die."

"That's not true," said the serpent. "You won't die. You will be like God if you eat this fruit."

Eve looked at the fruit.

It was beautiful.

She touched it.

It felt good in her hand.

Then she took a bite.

Eve gave Adam some of the fruit, too. He took a bite.

Suddenly they were both very much afraid. They had disobeyed God!

That evening when God came to visit Adam and Eve, they did not run to meet Him. They hid behind some bushes. They did not want God to see them. They did not want Him to know what they had done.

"Adam, Adam," God called. "Where are you?"

"I am afraid," said Adam. "I am hiding."

"Oh, Adam," said God, "did you eat the fruit that I told you not to eat?"

"Yes, but it was Eve's fault," said Adam. "She gave it to me."

"Eve," asked God, "what have you done?"

"It's not my fault," said Eve. "The serpent told me to do it."

12

God punished the serpent.

Then God made Adam and Eve leave their beautiful garden home. He said, "You cannot live here anymore. You will have to make a home for yourself somewhere else in the world, and finally you will die. But I shall never forget you. Someday, Someone will come to help you. Always remember that."

Adam and Eve did remember what God had said. They knew that God would keep His promise. They knew that God still loved them.

# CAIN AND ABEL

Genesis 4:1-16; Hebrews 11:1-4; 1 John 3:12

Adam and Eve had two boys. They called them Cain and Abel.

When they grew to be men, Cain became a farmer, and Abel took care of sheep.

One day Cain and Abel both got ready to give gifts to God. Cain made a pile of big stones and put some of his fruit on them. Abel made a pile of stones, too, and got some of his sheep ready to give to God.

Cain and Abel both gave their gifts to God, but God liked Abel's gift and did not like Cain's gift.

That made Cain very angry. "There!" he thought, "God loves Abel more than He loves me."

"Cain," said God, "why are you angry? You know, don't you, that if you do what is right, I will like your gift, too? Be careful and watch what you think and do."

But Cain did not listen. He was still angry. One day he said to his brother Abel, "Let's go out to the field."

"All right," said Abel.

When they were out in the field, Cain hit his brother Abel. He killed him.

"Cain, Cain!" called God. "Where is your brother Abel?"

"How should I know?" said Cain. "I don't have to take care of my brother, do I?"

"O Cain, what have you done?" said God. "Your brother is dead. You cannot stay here. You will not have a home anymore."

"My punishment is too hard," said Cain. "I will have to go from place to place and whoever finds me will kill me."

14

"No," said God, "I will put a mark on you, so that no one will kill you."

So Cain went away, but God kept people from hurting him.

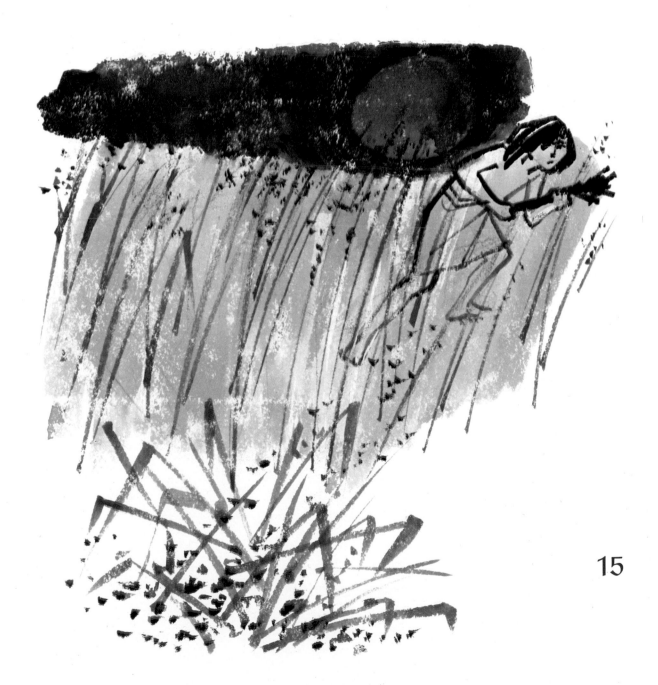

# GOD TAKES CARE OF NOAH

Genesis 6:5--9:19; 1 Peter 3:20; 2 Peter 2:5

After Adam and Eve had died and there were many people on this earth, there lived a man called Noah. He had three sons. Their names were Shem, Ham, and Japheth.

Noah loved God and tried to obey Him, but all other people on the earth did not love God. They did not obey Him. They did as they pleased. It grieved God very much.

One day God said, "Noah, very soon I will send a big flood of water on the earth to destroy the people. It will rain many, many days. I want you to build a boat so you and your family can float on the water. I will take care of you."

Noah obeyed God. He built a big, big boat. It had a roof and a door and a window.

Noah's neighbors laughed. "Why are you building a boat, Noah?" they called. "Are you going to sail on dry land?"

"God is going to send a great flood of water on the earth," said Noah. "Then I will need the boat."

Noah's neighbors did not believe him. They did not build any boats.

When Noah's boat was finished, God said, "Noah, it is going to start raining. Take your wife and your sons and their wives into the boat.

Take animals
and birds
and creeping things, two of every kind, into the boat. Take enough food for your family and all the animals, for it is going to rain a long time."

Noah obeyed God. He told his neighbors that the

16

rain would come, but they laughed. They did not listen to what Noah said.

When Noah and his family and the animals and the birds and the creeping things were in the boat, God closed the door to make sure they would be safe.

Then it began to rain.

It rained

and rained

and rained.

Soon there was so much water everywhere that it covered all the houses.

The boat with Noah and his family and all the animals in it floated away

over the treetops,

over the hills,

and over the mountains.

God watched over Noah and his family.

When it stopped raining and the earth was dry again, God said, "Noah, come out of the boat now.

Bring your wife,

bring your sons and their wives,

bring all the animals and birds and

creeping things, for the earth is dry again."

So Noah and his wife came out of the boat. Shem, Ham, and Japheth and their wives came out of the boat. All the animals and birds and creeping things came out of the boat. They were all glad when they saw the sun shining.

Noah said, "Thank you, God, for taking care of us during the rain."

"I will not let it rain this hard again," said God. "As long as the earth is here,

day will come after night,
   summer will come after winter,
      warm days will come after cold days;
and always food will grow after seed is sown. This is a
promise."

Then God said, "Look up at the sky, Noah. I have put

a sign there to help everyone remember what I have promised."

Noah looked up. He saw a beautiful rainbow in the sky!

And even today, when we see a rainbow, we remember that God keeps His promise, and that He takes care of us.

19

# ABRAHAM OBEYS GOD

Genesis 12:1-9; Hebrews 11:8

Abraham and his wife Sarah lived in a town called Haran.

Now God said to Abraham, "I want you to leave your home here in Haran and go to a country that I will show you. I will be good to you in that country and bless you so that you can be a blessing and a help to all the families of the earth."

Abraham went to his wife Sarah. "Sarah," he said, "God wants us to move to another country."

Abraham went to his nephew Lot. "Lot," he said, "God wants me to move to another country. Will you come with me?"

Lot decided to go with his Uncle Abraham and his Aunt Sarah. They all got ready.

Abraham had many sheep and goats and donkeys. He had many servants to help him take care of the animals. He had many things that needed to be packed.

But at last they were ready to go. Abraham and Sarah and Lot said good-bye to their friends and neighbors and started on the long trip to the country that God would show them.

Tap, tap, tap,

rap, rap, rap,

went the little feet of the donkeys and sheep and goats on the hard rocky road.

Some people rode on donkeys, and some people walked. On and on they went. When the sun was ready to set, everybody stopped and ate supper. Then they went to sleep. In the morning they started on their trip again.

"Uncle Abraham," said Lot, "I am tired of this trip. Why did we not stay at home?"

20

21

"I couldn't," said Abraham. "God told me to go. I love God and want to obey Him."

"But how will we know when we are where God wants us to be?" asked Lot. "Maybe we will just

      keep on going

         and going

           and going."

"No," said Abraham, "we won't keep on going and going and going. God told me He would show me the country where He wants me to go, and God always keeps His promises. He will tell us when to stop."

One day they came to a river. How would they get across?

"Maybe this is where God wants us to stop," said Lot.

"No," said Abraham. "God has not told me to stop yet."

So the people and sheep and goats and donkeys went

    splash,

        splash,

          splash,

across the river.

One evening they stopped under a big oak tree. That night God said, "Abraham, this is where I want you to live. This is the land that I will give to you and your children."

Abraham ran to tell Sarah and Lot. "We are there!" he cried. "God said this is the country in which we are to stay. This is the country God promised us."

They were all glad that the long trip was over. God had taken care of them and had shown them the way. Abraham said, "Thank you, God. Thank you!"

# ABRAHAM AND LOT

Genesis 13

Abraham and Lot made a home in the land that God had shown them.

Abraham became a very rich man. He had much silver and gold. He had many, many donkeys and sheep and goats and cows.

Lot had many donkeys and sheep and goats and cows, too.

All these animals needed a very big field to have enough grass to eat. Abraham's servants and Lot's servants were afraid their animals would not have enough.

25

When Abraham's servants took their animals out to the field in the morning, Lot's servants shouted, "Take your animals out of here! This grass belongs to Lot."

Abraham's servants shouted back, "No, we were here yesterday, and we are going to be here today. This grass belongs to Abraham."

One day Abraham heard his men and Lot's men shout-

24

ing at each other. It made him very sad. He did not want the men to quarrel. He went to Lot.

"Lot," he said, "you and I do not want to quarrel. And we do not want our servants to quarrel. There is enough grass in this land for your animals and for my animals. You go to one place, and I will go to another."

"That's all right with me," said Lot. "But how will we decide who goes where?"

"You choose first. I will take what is left," said Abraham. "If you want to go over there, I will go over here. If you want to go over here, I will go over there. It does not matter to me, as long as we don't quarrel about it."

Lot liked his Uncle Abraham's plan.

He looked this way,

he looked that way,

he looked all around.

Then he said, "Uncle Abraham, the grass is very green over there. I think that is where I will go."

"Good," said Abraham, "then I will move and take my animals to the other side."

After Abraham had moved, God called him. "Abraham," said God,

"Look this way.

Look that way.

Look all around you.

I will give you this land, as far as you can see. It will be yours and your children's."

Abraham believed God. He lived in the land that God had given him.

# ISAAC

Genesis 15:1-6; 17:15-21; 18:1-15, 21:1-7

Abraham and Sarah were very lonely. They had no children.

There were no boys in their home.

There were no girls in their home.

There was no baby.

Their tent house was very quiet.

God knew that Abraham and Sarah wanted a child to love. They wanted a child who would live after them.

One day God and Abraham were talking together. God said, "Abraham, I am going to give you something very wonderful!"

"Oh," said Abraham, "what are You going to give me? Really, I don't need anything since I have no son or daughter to give it to anyway."

"But that is just it," said God. "I am going to give you a son."

Abraham and Sarah knew that God always kept His promises,

so they waited,

and waited,

and waited for a baby boy.

But the baby did not come.

Had God forgotten His promise?

No, He had not forgotten.

One day, God came to see Abraham. He said, "I have not forgotten about your son, Abraham. He is going to be born next year, and I want you to call him Isaac."

Abraham and Sarah waited,

and waited,

and waited.

26

27

They were very old. How could old people have a baby? But there is nothing too hard for God.

God came to see Abraham again. Abraham was sitting in the door of his tent house.

"Abraham," said God, "where is Sarah?"

"She is in the tent," said Abraham.

"Well," said God, "I just want to tell you again. Get ready for a baby boy. When spring comes, he will be here."

And so he was! When spring came, Isaac was born.

Abraham and Sarah were very happy. Now they had a son of their own. God had kept His promise!

# JACOB AND ESAU

Genesis 25:19-34; 27:1-45; 31–33

When Isaac grew to be a man, he had two sons. Their names were Jacob and Esau.

One day Jacob took something that belonged to Esau, and Esau was so angry that he said, "I am going to kill my brother Jacob!"

When Jacob heard that, he was very much afraid. He ran away so his brother Esau could not find him.

After a long time God said to Jacob, "Jacob, I want you to go home again. I will take care of you."

So Jacob took his family and everything he had and started on the long trip home. He was still afraid of his brother Esau, but he did as God wanted him to do.

Jacob came closer and closer to his old home.

Now he was over the river he had to cross.

Now he was past the big pile of stones.

Now he was getting very close to where he would have to meet his brother Esau. What would Esau do to him when he saw him? Jacob was very much afraid.

He said to some of the men who were with him, "Go on ahead. Tell Esau I am coming home, and that I hope he is not angry with me anymore."

The men did as Jacob told them to. When they came back, Jacob asked, "Did you see my brother Esau?"

"Yes," said the men, "he is coming to meet you, and there are many, many men with him."

Now Jacob was sure that Esau was coming to hurt him. He became even more afraid.

Jacob said to God,

"God, You told me to go home again;

29

"You told me You would take care of me,
but I am still afraid.
Please do not let my brother Esau be angry with me anymore."

The next morning Jacob saw Esau coming toward him.

There were many men with him. Esau came closer and closer.

Jacob's heart pounded. He saw Esau was starting to run toward him. Would he hurt him?

But Esau was smiling. When Esau came to Jacob, he put his arms around him and kissed him. Esau had forgiven Jacob everything he had done to him. He was not angry with Jacob anymore.

Jacob and Esau were happy again. At last Jacob did not have to be afraid of his brother. Now he could go home.

# JOSEPH GOES TO EGYPT

Genesis 37

Jacob had a son called Joseph and a son called Benjamin and ten older boys.

The ten older boys did not like Joseph because he told their father when they were bad. They did not like Joseph because their father gave Joseph a pretty coat. They did not like Joseph because he told them he dreamed he would be their ruler.

One day Joseph heard his father calling him.

"Joseph."

"Here I am, Father," he answered.

"Joseph," said his father, "your brothers are watching the sheep at Shechem. I wonder how they are getting along. Go now and see whether they are all right."

Joseph started walking to Shechem. He was afraid his brothers would not be glad to see him.

When he came to Shechem, he looked and looked, but he could not see his brothers anywhere.

Finally, a man came along the road.

"Are you looking for someone?" he asked.

"Yes," said Joseph, "I am looking for my brothers. Can you tell me where they are watching their sheep?"

"Oh, I saw them," said the man. "I heard them say,

'Let us go to Dothan.'"

So Joseph went to Dothan.

At last, as he came over a hill, he could see the large flock of sheep. His brothers were sitting nearby. They saw him, but they did not wave. Joseph could tell that they were not happy that he had come.

When Joseph came nearer, his brothers shouted, "Ha, look who's here! Little Joseph, checking up on us! Tattletale! Tattletale! And what do you know, he is wearing his pretty coat!"

Joseph was afraid. Before he could run away, his brothers grabbed him, took off his coat, and threw him into a deep hole in the ground.

"Now you can't go back to Father and tell on us," they said.

Joseph did not know what to do. If his brothers would only let him go home!

But they would not.

Some men on camels rode by on their way to the country of Egypt. The brothers stopped the men and sold Joseph to them. The men took Joseph with them.

Joseph looked back. Soon he could no longer see his brothers. Then he could no longer see the hills where they kept the sheep. Everything was strange.

Joseph thought, "What will Father say when I don't come home?"

But Joseph knew God, and suddenly he remembered that God was with him.

34

Of course! God knew what was happening. When Joseph remembered that, he felt better. God was with him and so he did not need to be afraid.

# JOSEPH IN POTIPHAR'S HOUSE

Genesis 39

After a long trip, Joseph came to the land of Egypt.

He was lonesome for his father. He was lonesome for his younger brother Benjamin. He was even lonesome for his older brothers who had been angry with him and sent him away.

Joseph wished he could go home.

But he couldn't.

The men who brought Joseph to Egypt sold him to a man called Potiphar.

Potiphar had a big house. He told Joseph to take care of it for him.

Joseph was kind to Potiphar and all the people in his house.

Joseph did all the work that Potiphar asked him to do, the very best he knew how.

Joseph laughed and talked and sang because he knew that God was with him.

Potiphar liked Joseph. He liked the way Joseph did his work. He was glad that Joseph was always happy.

"Joseph," he said one day, "why is it that you are happy even when you are far from home?"

Joseph thought a while and then he said, "I think it is because I love God and God is always with me."

"So that is it," said Potiphar. "Yes, I see that you love God and that God is with you. You do everything so well. I'm happy to have you in my house."

Joseph was glad that Potiphar liked him.

But there was someone in the house who told Potiphar a lie about Joseph. It was Potiphar's wife.

She said, "Potiphar, Joseph is a bad man. He asked me to do something that is wrong."

That was not true, but Potiphar believed his wife. Potiphar became very angry. He had Joseph put into jail so he could not get out.

Joseph was sad. He had been kind. He had done his work well. Why was he being punished?

36

As Joseph thought about this, he remembered that God was with him. Of course! Even in jail Joseph did not need to be afraid.

# JOSEPH IN JAIL

Genesis 40; 41:1-45

Joseph was locked up in jail. He had to eat there.
He had to sleep there. He could not get out.

Joseph did not like being in jail.

He wished he could go out in the sunshine.

37

He wished he could feel the wind in his face.

He wished he could go and talk with his friends again.

But Joseph had to stay where he was. And even in jail Joseph knew that God loved him and was with him.

So Joseph was kind to all the people in the jail, and did all his work as well as he knew how.

The keeper at the jail liked Joseph very much. He let Joseph take care of the other men who were in the jail. But Joseph still wanted to get out.

One day a man who was also in the jail was allowed to go home.

"My friend," said Joseph to him, "when you get home, please go to Pharaoh and ask him to let me out of here. I have done nothing wrong, you know."

But when the man came home, he did not remember Joseph. He forgot all about him.

It was very hard for Joseph to wait so long. But he knew that God was right there with him, taking care of him.

After many, many days, the keeper at the jail called Joseph.

"Joseph, Joseph," he called. "Hurry! There are some men here to take you to Pharaoh. Pharaoh is calling you."

"Pharaoh!" said Joseph. "What does he want with me?"

"I don't know, I don't know," said the jail keeper. "Only hurry! Pharaoh does not like to be kept waiting."

Joseph rushed around. He shaved. He put on clean clothes. Then the men took him to Pharaoh's palace.

"Joseph," said Pharaoh, "the man who used to be in jail with you has just remembered you. He says you have done nothing wrong. He says you helped him, and he thinks you can help me. Will you work for me?"

"Oh, yes," said Joseph, "with God's help, I shall be glad to work for you."

And so, at last, Joseph was out of jail. He could see the sun and feel the wind, and he could go wherever he wanted to again.

Joseph was glad that no matter where he was, God was there, too.

# JOSEPH FORGIVES HIS BROTHERS

Genesis 42--46:7

After Joseph got out of jail, he was busy working for Pharaoh. But he often wondered,

"Will I ever see my father again?

Will I ever see my brother Benjamin?

Will I ever see my older brothers who sold me and sent me away from home?"

One day when Joseph was busy selling food to people who were hungry, he saw ten men coming to his house.

He thought he had seen those men before.

Joseph looked at them more closely.

Then he knew. The ten men were his brothers!

Joseph knew his brothers, but his brothers did not know him.

When the ten brothers came up to Joseph, they bowed down before him and said, "Please, sir, may we buy some food?"

Joseph pretended he did not know them. He did not tell them that he was Joseph. He said, "Well, I don't know. Where do you live?"

"We are from Canaan," they said.

"From Canaan!" said Joseph. "How do I know that you have not come to this country to hurt the people here?"

"Oh, no, sir," said the brothers. "We have only come to buy food. We have a father and a younger brother at home in Canaan."

"Oh, you do?" said Joseph. He was very glad to hear that his father was still alive. He was glad to hear about his brother Benjamin. He could hardly wait to hear more, but he did not tell his brothers that he was Joseph.

He said, "I will sell you some food now, but do not

40

41

ever come back again unless you bring your younger brother with you. When you bring him, I will know that you really have another brother and that you are telling the truth."

So the brothers went home. Joseph hoped they would soon come back again. He hoped they would bring his brother Benjamin to see him.

One day Joseph saw his brothers coming back to buy more food. And, sure enough, Benjamin was with them.

At first Joseph tried to pretend that he did not know them, but he was so glad to see his brothers that he could not keep his secret any longer. He cried, "I am Joseph! Don't you know me? How is my father?"

The brothers were so surprised and frightened they could not speak. They wondered if Joseph would punish them because they had been so mean to him.

"Do not be afraid," said Joseph. "I am your brother whom you sold into Egypt, but do not worry about that anymore.

"God sent me here so I could give you food and keep our family from starving. Hurry home now and get my father. Then we will all live here together where there is enough to eat."

And that is just what they did. The brothers went home and got father Jacob, and then they all lived in Egypt where Joseph was.

42

# BABY MOSES

Exodus 1:1--2:10

A long, long time after Joseph and his brothers had died, there lived in a little house by a river in Egypt, a father and a mother and their three children.

The little girl's name was Miriam.

The little boy's name was Aaron.

And the baby boy was so tiny that he didn't even have a name yet.

Mother and Father and Miriam and Aaron were happy for the baby at their house, but they were afraid that Pharaoh would find him. Pharaoh was a bad king who wanted to kill the baby boys.

At first Mother hid the baby in the back of the house.

"Miriam and Aaron," she said, "we do not want anyone to know that we have a baby. It is a big secret. You will not tell anyone, will you?"

"No," said Miriam, "I can keep a secret. I will not tell anyone."

"No," said Aaron, "I can keep a secret, too. I will not tell anyone."

So for a while the baby boy was safe. He was so tiny that Mother could hide him. But he grew very fast.

"What can I do?" thought Mother. "Someone is sure to hear the baby cry and tell the king."

But God was watching over the baby. God gave Mother a good idea.

Mother took a little basket made of reeds and grasses. She filled the cracks so no water could get in. Then she wrapped the baby in some blankets and put him into the basket.

Miriam and Aaron watched.

"Is that going to be the baby's bed?" asked Aaron.

43

"Yes," said Mother. "I have thought of a new place to hide him." Mother took the basket in her arms, and then she and Miriam and Aaron hurried to the river.

When they came to the river, Mother hid the basket in the tall grasses where the water was quiet and not deep.

"Miriam," said Mother, "Aaron and I have to go home now, but you stay here and watch what will be done to our baby."

Miriam hid in some bushes.

Soon she heard footsteps. The princess and some of her maidens were coming to bathe in the river. Would they find the baby?

"A basket!" Miriam heard the princess say. "How did it get here?"

Miriam saw the princess bend over the basket. "It must be one of the babies Pharaoh wants to kill," she said. "But I will not let him kill this baby. I want to keep him as my very own."

Quickly Miriam ran up to her and said, "Shall I get someone to take care of the baby for you?"

"Yes," said the princess. "Please do."

So Miriam ran to get her mother.

The princess put the baby into Mother's arms. "Take good care of the baby for me," she said. "Later he will live with me and be my son. I will call him Moses."

Now the baby had a name. Now they did not have to hide him anymore, because the princess would not let anyone hurt him. Mother took little Moses back to the house.

Miriam and Aaron had kept their secret well, but now they could tell everyone, "We have a little baby brother, and his name is Moses."

# THE ESCAPE FROM EGYPT

Exodus 3--14

Baby Moses grew
    and grew
        and grew.
Soon he was a big boy. After a while he became a big man.

One day when he was a man, he heard God call, "Moses, Moses!"

"Here I am," said Moses.

"Moses," said God, "I want you to do something for Me. Pharaoh is making My people work very hard. He is hurting them. I want you to go to Pharaoh. Ask him to let you take My people out of Egypt."

Moses did not want to go to Pharaoh and talk to him. So he said to God, "Please let someone else go and talk to Pharaoh. Please let someone else take Your people out of this country."

"No," said God, "I want you to go. Your brother Aaron will help you. I will tell you both what to say."

So Moses and Aaron did as God told them to do. They went to see Pharaoh.

"Listen," they said to Pharaoh, "God wants you to let His people go."

Pharaoh was very angry. "Who is God?" he shouted. "I will not do as He says! I will not let the people go. I will make them work harder for me than before!"

God heard Pharaoh. He said to Moses, "Tell Pharaoh if he will not let My people go, I will punish him."

So Moses told Pharaoh over and over again, "God says you must let His people go or He will punish you."

But Pharaoh would not listen to Moses. God began

47

to punish Pharaoh. He sent frogs to bother him. He sent many flies. He did many other things that Pharaoh did not like.

At last Pharaoh said to Moses, "All right. Take your people, and get out of here!"

Moses quickly led the people out of Egypt toward the sea. But before they had gone very far, Pharaoh and his soldiers came marching after them to bring them back to work.

"Moses, Moses!" the people cried. "Why did you bring us here to die? If we run forward, we will drown in the water that is in front of us. If we run back, Pharaoh will kill us."

"Do not be afraid," said Moses. "God will help us. Just wait and see what God will do."

Quickly God sent a strong wind to make a dry path through the water. Moses and the people walked safely to the other side. But when Pharaoh and his soldiers walked on the same path, the water rolled over them and drowned them.

God's people were free. Pharaoh could not hurt them anymore. Moses and all the people sang, "This is my God, and I will praise him."

# GOD GIVES MANNA

Exodus 16

After God had saved His people from Pharaoh, they kept on walking to a new country.

The boys and girls were tired,
the mothers and fathers were tired,
and Moses was tired.

At last they stopped for the evening.

"I am hungry, Mother," said one little girl.

"I am hungry, too," said a little boy.

"We are all hungry," said the other boys and girls.

"What shall we eat?" asked the fathers and mothers. "Our food baskets are all empty."

The fathers went to Moses. They said, "Moses, why did you bring us out here? Our children are hungry. We are all hungry. We have nothing to eat. What shall we do?"

Moses did not know what to do either. But God knew.

God said to Moses, "Tell the people to stop fussing. I know they are hungry, and I am going to send food so they have enough to eat."

"God is going to send food," Moses told the people.

Suddenly, many, many big birds called quail flew into the camp. The people caught them and cooked them for supper.

The next morning when it was light and the fathers and mothers and children came out of their tents, they saw something on the ground. It was little and white and round. They tasted it. MMM-mmm! It was good. It was sweet like cookies made with honey.

"What is it? What is it?" they asked.

49

"It is the food which God has given you to eat," said Moses. "God wants you to gather enough for one day."

So the fathers and mothers and children took baskets and ran out into the sunshine and picked up the food. They called it manna.

They had enough to eat for the whole day.

Each morning they went out to pick up the manna that God sent during the night.

And one day God told Moses to put a little bit of manna into a special jar to keep. He wanted grandparents and parents to remember to tell their children about the special food God gave them on their trip to the new country.

# GOD GIVES LAWS

Exodus 19; 20; 24:1-8

Moses and God's people were still on their long trip to a new country.

One day they camped near a tall mountain and Moses went up to talk with God. "Moses," said God,

"I helped the people get away from Pharaoh,

I made a way for them through the big water,

I gave them food to eat and water to

drink. They have seen all that I have done for them. Now tell the people this: 'If you will obey Me and do as I say, you will be My people. I will let you be My helpers all over the world.' "

Moses told the people what God had said.

"We will obey God," answered the people. "We will do everything He says."

When Moses told God this, God said, "Good. Tell the people to get ready. They must wear clean clothes. When the trumpet blows, I want them to come to the mountain so they can hear what I say."

The people quickly washed their clothing and got ready. Then they waited for the trumpet to blow.

They waited one day,

they waited another day,

they waited the third day.

They listened and listened, but all was quiet.

Then suddenly on the third day, they heard the trumpet blowing. Toot! Toot! Toot!

Everyone jumped up. Moses started walking to the mountain.

51

The grandparents followed him,
The parents followed him.
The boys and girls followed him.
Everyone went to the mountain to hear God speak.

The trumpet blew louder
      and louder
           and louder.

God said:

"I saved you from Pharaoh and brought you out of his country."

The people remembered.

"There is no other God. I want you to pray only to Me," said God. "Say My name only when you are talking to or about Me, and not just for fun or when you are angry."

The people listened carefully.

Then God said, "I want you to work six days, but on the seventh day I want you to rest and to think of Me."

The people listened carefully.

Then God said, "Children, obey your father and mother and love them."

The children listened carefully.

"Do not kill anyone," said God. "Husbands and wives, love each other. Do not take anything that belongs to someone else. Do not even want it. And don't ever say anything that is not true about your neighbors."

The people listened carefully. They remembered what God had done for them. They wanted to obey God and to be His helpers in the world. They were thankful that God had been so good to them, so they said all together, "All that God has asked us to do, we will do. We will obey Him."

God remembered what He had said.

The people remembered what they had said. They knew God would keep His promise, and that they would need to keep theirs.

# THE TENT CHURCH

Exodus 25--40; Numbers 6:22-27

God was glad that Moses and the people decided to be His people. God wanted to talk with them, and He wanted them to talk to Him.

So God called Moses.

"Moses," He said, "tell the people that I would like them to build a special tent church where we can meet and talk to each other. Let each one who wants to help build this tent, bring something.

We will need wood,

we will need gold and silver,

we will need blue and purple and red cloth. We will need many other things. Let each person who wants to help, bring wood or gold or blue cloth or purple or red cloth. Then you can start building. I will show you how to make the tent so you can fold it and take it with you as you travel to the new country."

Moses called all the people together.

The grandfathers and grandmothers came,

the fathers and mothers came,

the boys and girls came.

All of them wanted to hear what Moses would say.

"God wants us to build a special tent church where we can meet with Him," said Moses. "Everyone who wants to may help.

We will need wood,

we will need gold and silver,

we will need blue and purple and red cloth. We will need many other things. Bring whatever you want to bring."

54

The people hurried to their tents to see what they could give to help build the tent church.

Some brought wood,
some brought gold and silver,
some brought beautiful cloth.

They kept on bringing things until Moses said, "Do not bring any more wood or gold or silver or cloth. We have enough now. We will start building."

Soon everybody was busy. The men made the poles for the tent. The boys helped them. The women made curtains. The girls helped them embroider lovely patterns on the cloth. Everyone did what he could. At last the tent church was finished. It was beautiful!

The people could not see God Himself, but they saw a big cloud over the tent church. Then they knew God had come. They knew He was ready to listen to them and ready to talk to them. So they came to the tent church.

The grandfathers and grandmothers came,
the fathers and mothers came,
the boys and girls came.

They came to pray to God and to bring their gifts to Him.

When the church service was over, the priest blessed the people as God had told him to do. He said,

"The LORD bless you and keep you:
The LORD make his face to shine upon you, and be gracious to you:
The LORD lift up his countenance upon you, and give you peace."

Then the people went home. They were glad they had a place where in a special way they could meet God. They were glad that God was with them on their long trip to the new country.

# JOSHUA LEADS THE WAY

Joshua 3,4

God's people had almost come to the new country. Their long trip was nearly over. Moses had died. Now a man called Joshua became the leader of God's people.

Early one morning Joshua called out, "Time to get up, time to get up! We have a long way to go today."

The people sleeping in the tents heard him.

"Why do we have to get up so early today?" asked the children.

57

"We want to make it to the Jordan River before night," said the fathers. "Hurry up, now, we are almost ready to start."

So all the people got up quickly. Soon they were on their way.

When they came to the Jordan River, the children asked, "How are we going to cross the river?"

The fathers shook their heads. "We don't know," they said. "The river looks pretty deep. We hope Joshua will know what to do. God always told Moses what to do, but we don't know about Joshua."

Several days later, Joshua said, "Tomorrow God is going to do something very wonderful. Everybody get ready and watch for it."

The grandparents and parents and children were all excited. What would God do tomorrow? They could hardly wait.

The next morning Joshua called out, "Everybody come here, and listen to what God has told me to do."

First, Joshua told the priests to carry the box with God's written laws right into the river. The priests did not get their feet wet because God had made the water stop flowing and had made a dry path through the water.

The priests walked to the middle of the dried-up river and stood there while all the people walked across to the other side.

Then Joshua told twelve men each to pick one large stone from the bottom of the river and carry it to the shore.

When all the people were safely across, the priests came, too. Then God let the water in the river flow again. God's people had arrived in the new country.

Joshua took the stones that the men had brought from the river and put them in one big pile.

"What do those stones mean?" asked a boy.

"The stones are put there to help us remember that God led us through the river on dry ground," said his father. "They will tell all people that God is very strong, and they will help us remember to love God and obey Him."

# NAOMI AND RUTH

The Book of Ruth

Naomi was sad and lonesome. She lived in a strange country far away from her friends.

One day she said to her daughter-in-law Ruth, "I want to go home to Bethlehem where I used to live."

"All right, I'll go with you," said Ruth. "I'll stay wherever you stay."

So Naomi and Ruth started walking to Naomi's old home.

They walked
and walked
and walked.

They walked over the hills, they walked through the woods, they walked over the fields. They walked a long, long way.

At last they came to Bethlehem where Naomi used to live.

"Who is that old lady?" asked the people in Bethlehem when they saw Naomi coming down the street. "Can it be Naomi?"

"Yes, I am Naomi. I have come back because I was very lonesome so far away," said Naomi. "This is my daughter-in-law Ruth. She is going to live with me."

Naomi and Ruth moved into a little house in Bethlehem. But they had nothing to eat.

"Let me go and gather some grain in the field," said Ruth to Naomi. "Then we can make some flour and bake bread."

"Go, my daughter," said Naomi.

Ruth went out into the fields to gather grain. She brought the grain home. Naomi made flour and baked

60

61

bread. Now Naomi and Ruth had food to eat.

But Naomi was still sad.

There was no baby at her house.

There were no boys and girls at her house.

There was no one to call her "Grandma."

One day Ruth was married to a man named Boaz. By and by a baby boy was born to Ruth and Boaz.

Naomi's neighbors and friends came to see Naomi and said, "See, how good God has been to you? First He gave you Ruth, who loves you, and now He has given Ruth a tiny baby. The baby will call you 'Grandma' when he is bigger."

Naomi took the baby in her arms.

"Call the baby Obed," said Naomi's friends.

"That would be a good name," said Naomi.

"Yes," said Ruth and Boaz, "that would be a good name for our baby."

Grandma Naomi loved baby Obed. She took good care of him.

When Obed grew up, he had a little boy called Jesse; and when Jesse grew up, he had a little boy called David. David became a great king.

# GOD SPEAKS TO SAMUEL

1 Samuel 3--4:1

Once there was a boy called Samuel. Samuel lived with Eli, who was a priest in the church. Eli had two sons, but they did not obey God.

Samuel loved God and liked to help Eli take care of the church.

63

He liked to touch the soft curtains at the door.
He liked to look at the little flame in the lamp.
He liked to smell the sweet perfume.
But Samuel often wondered what God was like.
    He had not seen God,
        he had not touched Him,
            and he had not heard God speak.
Samuel wondered whether God would ever speak to him.

One day Eli said, "Samuel, I think you are big enough now to sleep in a room by yourself. Would you like to sleep in the room next to mine and take care of the box with God's written laws?"

"Oh, yes, yes," said Samuel.

He was glad that he could sleep in a room by himself and take care of the box with God's written laws. Samuel knew Eli was close by. And, besides, from his bed Samuel could see the little lamp that burned all night.

One night when Samuel was in bed, he heard a voice calling, "Samuel, Samuel!"

Samuel thought it was Eli. Quickly he ran to Eli and said, "Here I am, Eli. Did you call me?"

"Why, no," said Eli. "I didn't call you. Just go back to bed."

"That is strange," thought Samuel. "I was sure someone called me, and there is no one here but Eli."

When Samuel was back in his bed, he heard someone call again, "Samuel!"

Again Samuel jumped up and ran to Eli.

"Here I am," he said. "You called me."

"No," said Eli, "I didn't call you. Just go and lie down again."

Samuel went back to his room. As soon as he was in

**64**

bed, he heard the same voice calling, "Samuel, Samuel!"

Samuel ran to Eli again. "Here I am," he said. "I heard you call me."

Now Eli knew that God must be calling Samuel. So he said to Samuel, "Go and lie down. And if God calls you again, say, 'Speak to me, God. I am listening.'"

Samuel quickly ran back to his bed. Would God really, really talk to him?

He listened. It was very quiet.

And then he heard God calling him again, "Samuel, Samuel!"

Samuel answered quickly, "Speak to me, God. I am listening."

"I am going to punish Eli's sons for the wrong they have done," said God. "I want Eli to know it."

Then all was quiet again. Samuel lay quietly in his bed the rest of the night.

In the morning he got up and opened the doors of the church. He was afraid to tell Eli what God had said because he knew it would make Eli sad. But Eli called him.

"Samuel," said Eli, "what did God tell you last night?"

So Samuel told Eli everything.

That was the first time God talked to Samuel. After that God talked to Samuel often, and Samuel told the people what God had said. That way they all knew what God wanted them to do.

# OBEDIENCE IS BETTER THAN A GIFT

1 Samuel 15:1-31

After Samuel had become a man, a king called Saul ruled the country. One day God said to Samuel, "Go and tell King Saul to punish the people called Amalekites because they have been unkind. Tell Saul he must not bring home any of their sheep and donkeys and oxen, though."

Samuel went to King Saul and told him what God had said. "Be sure not to bring home any of the sheep and donkeys and oxen that belong to the Amalekites," he said. "God does not want you to do that."

King Saul took his men and punished the Amalekites, but he did not do exactly as God had told him to do. He and his men brought home many sheep and donkeys and oxen that they had taken from the Amalekites.

God saw what King Saul had done. He called Samuel. "Samuel," said God, "Saul has not obeyed Me. I am sorry I ever let him be king."

Samuel was very sad to hear that Saul had not obeyed God. He went to see Saul.

When Samuel came into the room, King Saul said, "I have done what God told me to do."

"Baa-a-a," said the sheep Saul had brought home.

"Hee-haw," said the donkeys Saul had brought home.

"Moo-o-o," said the oxen Saul had brought home.

"Oh," said Samuel, "God told you to punish the Amalekites. But He also said not to bring any sheep and donkeys and oxen home. What's all this

baaing

and hee-hawing

and mooing

66

that I hear outside?"

"Oh, we brought the best sheep and donkeys and oxen home to give to God as a present," said Saul.

"Saul, Saul," said Samuel, "why did you not obey God? Why did you take the sheep and donkeys and oxen?"

"But I did obey God!" said Saul. "I did everything God told me to, except that my men brought back a present for God."

"God would much rather have you obey Him than bring a present that He told you not to bring," said Samuel. "Since you have not obeyed God, He will not let you be king over His people very much longer. God will find another king, who will obey Him."

Saul bowed his head. He knew he had done wrong. He knew that God wants people to obey Him more than give gifts to Him.

# DAVID IS CHOSEN

1 Samuel 16:1-13

King Saul did not obey God and so God wanted His people to have a new king. He called Samuel.

"Samuel," said God. "I want you to go to Bethlehem to pray. Be sure to invite Jesse and his sons to be with you because one of Jesse's sons will be the new king. I will tell you when you get there which boy I have chosen."

So Samuel went to Bethlehem.

He invited the people to come to the meeting.

He especially invited Jesse to come and to bring all his sons.

When Jesse and his sons came, Samuel looked at them very carefully. He wondered which one of the boys God would want to be king.

The oldest boy came in. He was tall and strong and good-looking. Samuel thought, "Surely, he is the one whom God wants to be king."

"No, Samuel," said God. "He is not the one. I don't care what people look like. I care only whether they love and obey Me."

Then the second boy came in.

"Surely, this is the boy God wants to be king," thought Samuel.

"No, Samuel," said God. "This is not the one."

Then the third boy came in.

"Surely, this is the boy God wants to be king," thought Samuel.

**68**

"No, Samuel," said God again, "this is not the one."

So another one of Jesse's sons came in, and another, and another, and another, until all of them had stood before Samuel.

69

Each time God said to Samuel, "No, Samuel, this is not the boy I want to be king."

"This is strange," thought Samuel. "Something must be wrong."

"Jesse," Samuel said, "are these all the boys you have?"

"Well, no," said Jesse. "I have one more boy. His name is David. But he is very young, and he is out taking care of the sheep. He does not need to come, does he?"

"Oh, yes," said Samuel, "he must come. We will not start the meeting until David is here."

So Jesse said to one of his sons, "Quick! Run and get David. Samuel wants him to come, too."

The boy ran to the field to get David. When David came in, God said to Samuel, "Samuel, this is the boy. I want David to be king over My people."

Samuel poured some sweet-smelling oil on David's head and said, "David, this means that God wants you to be king over His people when you grow up."

David understood. David loved God and wanted to obey Him. He knew God was with him.

# DAVID AND HIS SHEEP

1 Samuel 17:34, 35

David loved his sheep.

When they were hungry, he took them to a place where there was green grass to eat.

When they were thirsty, he took them to quiet water where they could drink.

When they were tired, he took them to a shady place where they could rest.

When the sheep rested, David lay down in the grass, too.

He heard the birds s-singing in the trees.

He heard the wind wh-whispering in the grass.

He heard the water r-r-running over the stones. But one day he heard something else. He sat up and listened.

There was a rustle in the bushes, and before David knew what was happening, a big lion jumped out and grabbed one of the lambs.

The other sheep were afraid and ran in all directions.

David was up, quick as a flash. He grabbed a big stick and killed the lion.

Then David took the lamb in his arms.

He petted it,

he talked to it until it stopped crying and settled down in his lap. The other sheep came back and lay down near David where they knew they were safe.

David took out his harp and played.

It sounded like birds s-singing in the trees.

It sounded like wind wh-whispering in the grass.

It sounded like water r-r-running over the stones.

The sheep fell asleep. David lay down in the grass and thought about God, because God seemed very close to him.

# DAVID AND JONATHAN

1 Samuel 16:14-23; 18:1, 2

Jonathan was a prince. He lived in a palace with his father, King Saul. But Jonathan was sad. He saw that his father was not at all happy. Often King Saul just sat and would not talk to Jonathan or anyone else.

One day King Saul's servants said, "King Saul, will you let us bring you a man who can sing and play on an instrument to cheer you up?"

Jonathan hoped his father would say yes.

"I will be glad to have such a man around here," said King Saul. "Look for someone who can play well and bring him to me."

73

"I already know a man like that," said one of the servants. "His name is David. He is a shepherd and lives with his father Jesse in the town of Bethlehem."

"All right, then," said King Saul. "Send some messengers to Jesse and ask him to let his son David come to me."

Jonathan was excited. What would David be like? Would he be able to help his father be happy again?

At last the messengers came back with David. Soon he was standing before King Saul and Jonathan.

"My boy," said King Saul to David, "please sit down and play something on your instrument."

David sat down. He started playing.

The music sounded like birds s-singing in the trees.

The music sounded like wind wh-whispering in the grass.

The music sounded like water r-r-running over the stones.

Jonathan looked at his father. King Saul was listening. He had a smile on his face.

Jonathan looked at David. David looked happy. Jonathan liked David.

When David stopped playing, King Saul said, "Good, good. I liked that, David. You must play again for me. But now I will let Jonathan take you to your room. We want you to stay with us."

Jonathan jumped up. "Come on, David," he said. "Let's go."

74

Jonathan and David became very good friends. And always when King Saul was sad, David played for him to make him happy again. Jonathan was glad that David had come.

# SOLOMON BUILDS GOD'S HOUSE

2 Samuel 7:1-17; 1 Kings 5, 6, 8

After King Saul died, David became king. David loved God and tried to obey Him. He wanted to build a beautiful house where he and the people could pray to God.

But God said to David, "Why do you want to build a house for Me? I have never asked you to. And, anyway, there is too much war going on around you. Later on I will let your son build Me a house where the people can hear My name and worship Me."

So David's son Solomon built a house of God after David had died.

One day God said, "Solomon, now about this house you are building--as long as you obey Me, I will live among My people and never leave them."

Solomon told the people to bring big stones.

He told them to bring shiny wood.

He told them to bring gold to cover the walls. He wanted the house to be beautiful to show God that he loved Him.

At last the house was finished.

King Solomon called all the priests.

He called the grandparents.

He called the parents and children.

"Come," he said, "we want to thank God for being so good to us. We want to ask Him to hear us when we pray to Him in this house."

So all the priests came.

All the grandparents came.

All the parents and children came.

King Solomon knelt down and lifted his hands up to God. He prayed, "We thank You, God, for loving us. We thank You for giving us all the things that You promised.

"We know that You are far too great to be only in this house. But please hear us when we come here to pray.

"Forgive us when we do wrong.

"Hear us when we ask for rain so our crops may grow.

"When we are sick, make us well again.

"And, please, dear God, when a man comes from a faraway country to pray in this house, hear him also so

that all people in the world may learn to know You."

Then King Solomon stood up. He knew God had heard him. The priests and the grandfathers and grandmothers and fathers and mothers and children knew God heard him.

For seven days they had a great celebration. Then everyone went home. They were glad that God had been so good to them.

# ELIJAH IN ZAREPHATH

1 Kings 17:1-16

Once there was a prophet called Elijah. For a while he lived near a little creek, but he could see that the creek was drying up. There had been no rain for a long time. Very soon he would have no water to drink.

Elijah didn't know what to do.

One day God said, "Elijah, do not stay here any longer. Go to the little town called Zarephath. I have told a woman who lives there to give you food to eat and water to drink."

So Elijah went to Zarephath. When he came near to the town, he saw a woman gathering sticks. He knew this must be the woman about whom God had told him.

So Elijah called to the woman, "Please, give me a drink of water. I am very thirsty."

The woman went to get some water.

Elijah called after her, "And, please, could you also bring me something to eat?"

The woman turned around and looked at Elijah. She was very sad.

"Sir," she said, "I would be glad to bring you something to eat, but I have no bread myself. I have only a small handful of flour and a wee bit of oil. I was gathering sticks to make a fire to bake a little bread for my boy and me. After we eat the bread, we will have nothing more. Then we will die."

"No," said Elijah, "you will not die. God told me that there will always be a little flour in your flour box and a little oil in your jar until it rains again and new wheat can grow. Go, bake a little bread and bring it to me. Then there will be enough for you and your son, too."

Elijah saw the woman turn and go to her house. Would she do as he said? Would she bake the bread and bring it to him, or would she and her little boy eat it themselves?

Elijah sat down to wait.

After a while Elijah saw the woman come running out of her little house.

The woman was laughing and crying, she was so excited.

"I baked the bread as you said, sir," she called. "Here it is, and here is some water. And what you said is true. There is still flour in my flour box and oil in my jar. There is enough to bake bread for us all."

Elijah was glad that God had given the woman flour and oil so she and her little boy could eat. He was glad that she had shared what she had with him.

# NAAMAN

2 Kings 5:1-15

Naaman was a great man in the country of Syria, but the time came when everyone in the house of Naaman was very sad. Naaman was sick with leprosy and no one could help him.

Naaman's wife cried. The little girl who was her servant cried. They loved Naaman dearly and wanted him to get well again, but no one knew what to do.

All at once the little girl said to Naaman's wife, "I know what we should do. There is a prophet called Elisha who lives in the country where I come from. He knows God, and he will be able to make Naaman well again."

Naaman's wife ran to Naaman. She said, "My little girl helper says there is a man called Elisha who knows God. Quick, you must go to Elisha. He can make you well again."

Naaman was glad there was someone who could help him. He said to his servants, "Pack food and clothing for the trip. Get the horses ready. Shine up the chariots in which we will ride."

Soon Naaman and his servants clattered down the road. Round and round went the chariot wheels. Clop, clop, clop, went the horses' hooves. Naaman's wife and her little servant girl waved to Naaman as they saw him go.

"I hope Elisha can help him," said Naaman's wife.

"I know he will," said the little girl.

After a long trip, Naaman and his servants drove up to Elisha's door.

Before Naaman could get out of his chariot, a messenger came out of Elisha's door.

"Naaman," said the messenger, "Elisha says you should

80

go and wash yourself in the Jordan River seven times and then you will be well again."

This made Naaman very angry. "I thought Elisha himself would come out," he said. "I thought Elisha would call to God and ask Him to make me well. I thought he would do something. I am not going to bathe in that muddy old water in the River Jordan. I am going home!"

But one of Naaman's servants said, "Naaman, why don't you do as Elisha says? Why don't you at least try? If it were something hard, you would do it."

Naaman listened to this. He went down to the Jordan River.

He dipped himself into the water again and again as he counted, "One, two, three, four, five, six--seven!"

There, he had washed himself seven times. As he came out of the water, Naaman saw that he was well again!

Quickly they went back to Elisha's house. This time Elisha asked them to come in.

"Elisha," said Naaman, "now I know that there is no God like your God. From now on I am going to love and obey Him."

Then Naaman and his servants drove home. Round and round, faster and faster, went the wheels of their chariots. Clop, clop, clop, faster and faster, went the horses' hooves.

Naaman's wife and her little servant girl saw them coming and ran to meet them. How happy they all were that God made Naaman well again!

# A ROOM FOR ELISHA

2 Kings 4:8-11

The Prophet Elisha, who made Naaman well, walked from place to place to help people and tell them what God wanted them to do.

One day Elisha went to a town called Shunem. "Come to our house and have dinner with us," said a rich lady who lived there.

Elisha was glad to go to the lady's house for dinner. He had a good time visiting with her and her husband.

After that, whenever Elisha walked through the town of Shunem, he stopped at the lady's house. The lady and her husband were always glad to see him.

One day the lady said to her husband, "I can see that Elisha is a good man and that he obeys God. He must get very tired walking so much. Just look how often he comes through this town. Why don't we build a special little room for him on top of our house. Then he can always rest there before he goes on."

"Now that is a good idea," said the lady's husband. "Let's do that."

Soon the lady's husband and the carpenters were busy building an extra room on the flat roof of the house.

They carried up stones for the walls,

they carried up boards for the door,

they carried up everything they needed to build a room for Elisha.

At last the room was finished.

The lady and her husband put a bed into the room so Elisha could sleep there. They put a chair into the room for him to sit on. They put a table and a lamp into the room so he could read and write.

They could hardly wait to see what Elisha would say when he saw the special room they had built for him.

At last one day the lady saw Elisha coming down the road. It was hot and dusty, and Elisha was walking slowly.

The lady called her husband. "Elisha is coming!" she said, all excited. She ran to get a pitcher of cold water to put on the table so Elisha could have a cold drink when he came.

Then the lady and her husband stood at the door of their home. "We have a surprise for you," they said when Elisha got there. "You must come up and see it."

The lady led the way up the steps on the outside of the house. Her husband followed with Elisha. Then the lady said, "Come in, Elisha, this is your room. Whenever you come through Shunem, come in to rest and stay as long as you like."

Elisha walked into the room. It was cool there. He sat down on the chair and drank some water. He was very thirsty and tired. "Thank you," he said with shining eyes, "thank you."

The lady and her husband saw that Elisha liked their surprise.

Every time Elisha came through Shunem he went to his little room and rested.

85

God saw that people who had big houses and good food and many clothes were doing bad things to get even more houses and food and clothing. God saw the rich people take things from the poor people who had very little, so that they themselves could have more.

God did not like that.

He called Amos.

Amos was out on the field taking care of his sheep, but he heard God calling him.

"Amos," said God,

"go and tell the people to stop cheating.

Tell them to stop lying.

Tell them to stop taking things that do not belong to them. I want them to do that which is right. If they do not, I will punish them. I will take away their beautiful homes. I will send them away until they learn to listen to Me."

Amos did as God told him to do. He went out into the street and called, "Listen all you people!

God knows you are cheating.

God knows you are lying.

God knows you are taking things that do not belong to you. If you do not stop doing these things, He will punish you. He will send you away from your homes until you let other people have what belongs to them, and until you learn to listen to God."

Amaziah, the priest, heard Amos preaching in the street. He was angry. He ran to Amos and said, "You go on home! We do not want to hear what you are saying. We do not want you around here."

But Amos said, "I cannot go home. God told me to tell the people that He is going to punish them if they do not listen to Him. I am going to obey God."

God heard what Amos was saying.

He said, "Amos, now the people do not obey Me.
They take things that do not belong to them.
They cheat so they can have nicer houses.
They lie so they can get more money.
I will have to send them away. But someday they will learn to listen to Me, and then I will let them come home again."

87

# THE LOST BOOK

2 Kings 22:1–23:3

Josiah was eight years old. One, two, three, four, five, six, seven, eight years. Something very special happened to Josiah when he was eight years old. He became king.

Josiah wanted to be a good king. He wanted to obey God and do whatever God wanted him to do.

When Josiah grew up, he thought one of the things God would want him to do was to fix up the house of God. It was called a temple.

There were holes in the floor,
there were cracks in the walls,
and in some places the roof leaked.
So Josiah called his carpenters.

"Fix the floor in the temple," he said. "Mend the cracks in the walls. Fill the holes in the roof. We want a beautiful temple."

Soon the helpers were busy working. Bang, bang, bang! Whop, whop, whop!
They fixed the floor.
They mended the cracks in the walls.
They filled the holes in the roof.

The priest was busy in the temple, too. His name was Hilkiah. He thought this was a good time to clean up the shelves and dark corners.

One day he found a book that was covered with cobwebs and dust. He opened it carefully and started reading.

"Shaphan, Shaphan!" he called to his helper. "Look what I found."

Shaphan came running. "What is it?" he asked.

"I have found a book," said Hilkiah. "In it are written the laws God gave us many years ago."

88

Shaphan was excited. "We must take the book to King Josiah at once," he said. "The king will want to know about it."

"Yes," said Hilkiah, "take the book to the king and read it to him."

Shaphan held the book very carefully and carried it to King Josiah.

"Hilkiah has given me a book," Shaphan said to King Josiah.

"Oh," said King Josiah, "read it to me."

So Shaphan started reading.

"What!" cried King Josiah. "Read those words again."

Shaphan read the words again.

"It is the book that was lost," said Josiah. "It tells us what God wants us to do. Read all of it to me."

As Shaphan read God's laws in the book, King Josiah became very sad.

"We have not done what God wants us to do," Josiah said. "We have fixed up the temple, but we have not loved each other as God says we should. We have not obeyed God's laws."

Then King Josiah said, "Call the people and tell them to come to the temple. I want them to hear what God says in this book."

Soon the priests and teachers
and grandfathers and grandmothers
and fathers and mothers
and boys and girls
were on their way to the temple.

King Josiah met them there. He stood straight and tall. Josiah opened the book and read with a loud voice so everyone could hear.

Then King Josiah prayed. All the people prayed with him.

"Forgive us, God," said King Josiah. "We did not know until now what You wanted us to do. Now that we know, we will try with all our hearts to obey You and love each other."

"Yes," said all the people. "We will obey God."

90

# JEREMIAH OBEYS GOD

Jeremiah 38:1-13

Jeremiah was a prophet. He said what God wanted him to say.

"You have not obeyed God," Jeremiah said to the people. "God is good to you, but you do not love Him. You do not even talk to Him. God will let other people punish you. They will burn your houses."

The princes did not like what Jeremiah said, so they took ropes and lowered Jeremiah into a cistern. The cistern was a deep hole. It was dark and damp and muddy.

As Jeremiah stood in the hole, he sank deeper and

91

deeper into the mud.

Jeremiah had nothing to eat.

He had nothing to drink.

He would surely die if no one came to help him.

But Jeremiah had a good friend from the country of Ethiopia. His name was Ebedmelech. When Ebedmelech heard that Jeremiah was in the cistern, he went straight to the king.

"My lord the king," he said, "it is not right that Jeremiah was thrown into the cistern.

He has nothing to eat.

He has nothing to drink.

He will die in the mud."

The king said, "Ebedmelech, you are right. Take some men with you and lift Jeremiah out of the cistern before he dies."

So Ebedmelech took some men with him and ran to help Jeremiah. He knew Jeremiah would be very weak. He knew if he pulled Jeremiah out with ropes, it would hurt his arms. So he took old rags and worn-out clothes along. He tied ropes around them and let them down to Jeremiah.

"Jeremiah," he called. "Put the rags and clothes under your arms and then tie the rope around your body."

Jeremiah did as Ebedmelech told him.

Then Ebedmelech and the men pulled Jeremiah up out of the cistern.

At last Jeremiah was free. Even though the princes might be angry with him again, Jeremiah kept on telling the people what God wanted them to do. He said what God wanted him to say. He was a true prophet.

# DANIEL AND HIS FRIENDS

Daniel 1:1-20

Daniel and his three friends were far from home. King Nebuchadnezzar had taken them away from their country and had brought them to his palace. They wondered what would happen next.

"Daniel," whispered his friend Hananiah, "what do you think King Nebuchadnezzar will do to us?"

"I don't know," said Daniel. "Sh-sh, someone is coming."

A man walked up to them and said, "I am Ashpenaz. I am the king's servant. King Nebuchadnezzar wants to see you; but before I take you to him, I want to know your names.

"What is your name?" Ashpenaz asked Daniel.

"Daniel."

"Daniel!" said Ashpenaz, "That is a funny name! It will never do. We do not have names like that here. I will call you Belteshazzar."

Daniel did not want another name. He did not like to be called Belteshazzar.

"And what is your name?" Ashpenaz asked Hananiah.

"Hananiah."

Ashpenaz shook his head. "I will call you Shadrach."

Then Ashpenaz turned to another of Daniel's friends. "What is your name?" he asked him.

"Mishael."

"You will be called Meshach," said Ashpenaz.

Mishael did not like to be called Meshach.

"What is your name?" Ashpenaz asked another of Daniel's friends.

"Azariah."

93

"Well, well," said Ashpenaz. "Let's see. I will call you Abednego."

Azariah looked down. He did not like to be called by another name.

But before Daniel and his three friends could think about their new names, Ashpenaz took them to the king.

King Nebuchadnezzar sat in a big, big room. At first Daniel and his friends could hardly see him, he seemed so far away.

When they came closer, Ashpenaz said to the king, "O King, here are the four young men from the land of Judah that you wanted to see. Their names are Belteshazzar, Shadrach, Meschach, and Abednego."

"Hmm," said the king. "They are good-looking. Give them the food I eat and the wine I drink. After three years bring them back to me. I want to see if they are growing strong and healthy and if they are learning to be my servants."

Ashpenaz bowed before the king. He took the young men back to their room.

Daniel and his three friends were very sad.

"Ashpenaz changed our names," said Hananiah.

"Now King Nebuchadnezzar wants us to eat the kind of food and drink the kind of wine that our mothers and fathers told us God does not want us to eat and drink," said Mishael.

Azariah said, "They want us to belong to King Nebuchadnezzar, not to God."

"Yes," said Daniel, "but no matter what they call us, we will still be Daniel and Hananiah and Mishael and Azariah. And no matter what they ask us to do, we will still obey God."

And that is exactly how it was. Daniel and Hananiah and Mishael and Azariah grew to be big, strong men who talked with God and belonged to Him.

95

# NEHEMIAH

Nehemiah 1--6:16

Nehemiah saw that the city of Jerusalem was in ruins.
The trees were dead,
the houses had tumbled down,
and the wall that used to be around
the city had been pushed over. Nehemiah wondered what
he could do to make Jerusalem beautiful and whole again.

He called several men.

"Sh," he said. "I'm going to tell you something. Don't
tell anyone. It is a secret. Tonight, when it is dark so our
enemies can't see me, I want to ride around the city of
Jerusalem to see what can be done to build it again. Will
you come with me?"

The men nodded their heads. They did not say a word.

That night when everyone was asleep, Nehemiah and
the men went to see what could be done to build a wall
around Jerusalem again so no enemies could get in.

The feet of the animal on which Nehemiah rode did
not make much noise. The feet of the men who were with
Nehemiah did not make much noise. The enemies did not
hear them.

Nehemiah went to the wall. It was broken down. The stones lay around on the grass.

Nehemiah went to the gates. They had been burned. There were only black ashes left.

Nehemiah went to the king's pool, but there was no water in it. There were so many stones lying around that they could not go any farther.

Nehemiah and the men who were with him went back to their house.

The next morning Nehemiah called the people,
he called the priests,
he called the princes.

Nehemiah said, "You can see that we are in trouble. The walls around Jerusalem are broken down. The gates are burned. Our enemies can come into the city anytime. Come, let us build the wall again. God has sent me here to help you."

"Yes," said the people.

"Yes," said the priests.

"Yes," said the princes.

"Let us all work together to build the wall around Jerusalem again."

So they did. They all worked hard. Their enemies laughed at them but the people went right on building.

Then the enemies planned to come and fight against them. The people were afraid, but Nehemiah said to them, "Don't be afraid. Remember how great and strong God is. He will help us. Watch, watch so no enemies can get in, and keep on building."

The people did as Nehemiah said. They prayed and worked and watched.

At last the wall around Jerusalem was finished and the gates closed. Now no enemies could get in.

Nehemiah and all the people were glad. Their enemies said, "God must have helped them to finish the job. They could never have done it alone."

# JONAH

The Book of Jonah

"Jonah, Jonah," called God one day, "I see the people in the city of Nineveh are doing very bad things. I want you to go there and tell them that I will punish them."

Jonah heard God, but he did not say anything. He kept very quiet. He did not want to go to Nineveh.

"I will pretend I did not hear God, and run away before He calls again," thought Jonah.

Jonah hurried to Joppa and got on a big ship. Soon the ship was sailing to faraway Tarshish. Jonah lay down on his bed to sleep. "God will not find me here," he thought.

But God watched Jonah. He saw him on the ship, lying on his bed, fast asleep, when he should have been going to Nineveh.

So God sent a big storm to wake him up. Jonah knew very well that God was sending the storm, but still he would not listen.

Then God let the people on the ship tell Jonah that he had better talk with God. Still Jonah would not listen.

The men on the ship threw Jonah into the water, so God sent a big fish to swallow Jonah. Perhaps now Jonah would listen.

When Jonah was in the big fish, he remembered God and prayed to Him for help. God heard him. God spoke to the fish, and the fish spit Jonah out again on the dry land.

"Jonah, Jonah!" called God again. "I told you to go to Nineveh. Remember?"

This time Jonah listened. He went to Nineveh, but

99

he went very, very slowly. He still did not want to go.

He still did not want to talk to the people in Nineveh.

At last Jonah came to Nineveh. He walked along the streets and called, "Listen, all you people, God is going to punish you."

The fathers and mothers listened.

The boys and girls listened.

Even the king listened.

They were all sorry for the bad things they had done. They asked God to help them do what was right.

God loved the people in Nineveh very much. He saw that they were doing what was right now, and so He

decided not to punish them.

That made Jonah angry. He hated the people in Nineveh. He was sorry that God did not punish them.

"Oh, God!" he said. "This is exactly what I thought would happen. This is why I did not want to go to Nineveh. Why are You letting these people go without punishing them?"

God said, "I am surprised at you, Jonah! Why should I punish them now when they are sorry for what they have done, and obey Me? There are more than a hundred and twenty thousand people and many animals in Nineveh. I am sorry for them."

# GOD CHOOSES MARY

Luke 1:26-38

God told the Prophet Jonah that He felt sorry for the people in Nineveh. He had told other prophets many times that He loved all people and wanted to help them.

One day God called the Angel Gabriel.

"Gabriel!"

Gabriel came and stood before God.

"I want you to do something very special for Me," said God.

Gabriel came closer. He was eager to hear what God would tell him.

"Gabriel," said God, "the right time has come. I am going to send My Son to help people to love Me and each other.

Go now to the town of Nazareth,
to the home of a girl called Mary,
who is going to be married to a man
called Joseph. I want you to tell Mary that I have chosen her to be the mother of My Son."

Gabriel did as God said.

Gabriel went to Nazareth,
he went to Mary's home,
he found Mary, and said to her, "Hello, Mary, God is with you!"

Mary looked up. Gabriel could see that Mary was afraid. She could not understand why an angel had come to see her.

102

Gabriel said to Mary, "Do not be afraid, Mary. God has sent me to tell you a wonderful secret. He has chosen you to be the mother of His Son, who will be born as a tiny baby. God wants you to name the baby Jesus."

Now Mary was no longer afraid of the angel. God had
sent him, and she could talk to him!

"Tell God that I want to do everything He wants me
to do," Mary said to the angel. "I shall be glad to be the
mother of the baby Jesus and take care of Him."

# JESUS IS BORN

Luke 2:1-7; Matthew 1:21

Mary remembered what the angel had told her. She was glad that God had chosen her to be the mother of His Son. She remembered that the baby's name was to be Jesus.

Mary waited for the baby Jesus.

Mary's husband, Joseph, waited for the baby Jesus.

One day Joseph said, "Mary, the king in Rome wants to count all the people in the land. We shall have to go to the town of Bethlehem to be counted."

"To Bethlehem!" said Mary. "O Joseph! How can we? What if the baby should come?"

"Yes," said Joseph, "it worries me, but the king says we have to go. Maybe the baby will not be born until we get back."

So Mary and Joseph started out on the long trip to Bethlehem.

They walked
        and walked
                and walked.

Sometimes Mary rode on a donkey, but she became very tired. Would they ever get there?

At last Mary and Joseph saw the houses of Bethlehem.

"We are almost there, Mary," said Joseph. "Try to walk just a little bit farther. It won't be long before we get to the hotel."

But there were many, many other people who had come to Bethlehem to be counted. They all wanted a place to sleep.

When Mary and Joseph came to the hotel or inn, it was full of people. There was no more room.

Mary and Joseph turned away and went slowly down the street. Where could they stay?

When they came to a house, Joseph knocked on the door.

Knock! Knock! Knock!

A man came out.

"May we stay here for the night?" asked Joseph. "My wife is very tired."

"No," said the man, "we have no room at our house."

Mary and Joseph went on to the next house. They just had to find a place to sleep.

Knock! Knock! Knock!

A man opened the door.

"May we stay here for the night?" asked Joseph again.

The man shook his head. "There is no room at our house," he said. "I am sorry, but we can't take you in."

"Joseph," whispered Mary, "I cannot go any farther. Please, please, any little place will do."

When the man saw how tired Mary was, he said, "There is a place where we keep our animals. Would you like to stay there?"

"Yes, oh, yes," said Mary.

"Thank you," said Joseph.

The man took Mary and Joseph to the place where the cows and the donkeys and the sheep slept. It was quiet there, and warm.

Mary and Joseph were happy to have a place at last where they could rest. Mary lay down on the hay. In the quietness God seemed very near. He was! That night Mary's baby was born. Mary and Joseph called Him Jesus just as the angel had told them to do.

Mary wrapped the baby in long strips of soft cloth called swaddling cloths. She held Him while Joseph got a little bed ready for Him in a manger. Baby Jesus was cozy and warm on His little bed of hay.

Mary and Joseph were glad that at last the baby was born. God had kept His promise.

106

# THE SHEPHERDS

Luke 2:8-20

On the same night that Jesus was born in Bethlehem, shepherds were watching their sheep in the fields nearby.

All was dark and quiet.

The sheep were huddled together and fast asleep.

The shepherds were sitting close together, too. It was a night like any other night.

But then something happened.

Suddenly the dark night was all gone. Suddenly it was as light as day.

The shepherds jumped up. They could not believe their eyes. In the great and shiny light they saw an angel coming toward them. They were very much afraid.

"Do not be afraid, shepherds!" said the strong and joyful voice of the angel. "Why, this is the most wonderful night there ever was!

"I bring you good news of a great joy which will come to all people. The baby Jesus is born! He is the Savior
who will help the sad people,
the lonely people,
the people who are doing wrong.
He will show all people the way back to God. You will find the baby in Bethlehem, lying in a manger."

And suddenly there was not only one angel, but there were so many, many angels that the whole sky seemed full of them. And they were all singing a great and wonderful song. They said, "Glory to God in the highest! And on earth peace among men with whom he is pleased."

Then the angels went back to heaven. Before the shepherds knew what had happened, the night was dark and quiet again.

107

The shepherds looked and looked. They could not believe that the angels were gone. Then they remembered what the angel had said.

"The baby!" they said. "Let us go and see the baby."

The shepherds ran to Bethlehem as fast as they could go. And there they found Mary and Joseph and the baby Jesus lying in a manger.

"How did you know the baby was here?" asked Joseph softly.

"The angels told us," said the shepherds. "The angels, a whole skyful, came down from heaven to tell us. They

said this baby is the Savior who will
    help the sad people,
      the lonely people,
        the people who are doing wrong."
    Mary and Joseph listened carefully. Other people
heard the shepherds. They came and listened carefully,
too. They were all glad that God sent angels to tell them
that this baby was very special.

    Then the shepherds went back to their sheep. They
thanked God for all that they had heard and seen.

109

# ANNA AND SIMEON

Luke 2:25-38

Ever since God promised to send His Son Jesus into the world, many, many people waited for Him.

"When will He come, dear God?" asked Simeon, an old, old man.

"When will He come?" asked Anna, an old, old lady.

Simeon and Anna did not know that baby Jesus had been born in Bethlehem. God wanted them to know that He kept His promise, and that His Son had come.

One day God said to Simeon, "Simeon, you have been waiting a long time for Jesus. Go to the temple church today. Baby Jesus will be there."

Simeon walked to the temple as fast as he could. He stood by the big door where he could see the people come and go.

Many people walked past him. Simeon wondered how he would ever know the baby Jesus.

"God," he prayed, "please tell me which one is Jesus. I do not want to miss seeing Your Son, now that He is so near."

Simeon looked at every one coming into the temple. There were big men and little men; there were big women and little women. There were many middle-sized men and women. Some had babies with them and some did not.

Then Simeon saw a man and woman come through the door. The woman had a little baby in her arms. The man was Joseph and the woman was Mary. They were bringing baby Jesus to the temple to thank God for Him.

"Simeon," said God. "Here is the baby you have been waiting for."

Simeon walked up to Mary and Joseph. He took baby

110

Jesus in his arms and looked at Him for a long time. Then
he said, "O God, now that I have seen this child, I shall
be happy to die. Thank you for sending the One who will
help all the people in the world to know You."

Simeon put the baby gently back into Mary's arms.
Then he blessed Mary and Joseph and said to Mary, "When
Jesus grows up, many people will love Him and many
people will hate Him. You, Mary, will be sad because of
what people will do to Him."

Just then the old, old lady Anna came up to Mary
and Joseph. God told her, too, that the baby in Mary's
arms was the One she was waiting for.

Anna said, "Thank you, God, thank you for sending
baby Jesus!" Then she told all the people who had been
waiting for Jesus, "See, God has kept His promise. He
has sent the One who will show us the way to God."

111

# THE WISE MEN

Matthew 2:1-12

Now when Jesus was born, a beautiful big star shone in the sky.

"Look!" shouted one man to another. "Look at that star!"

"Where? Where?" Soon many men were looking up at the beautiful new star.

"I think that star belongs to a very special king, and it is there to tell us that the king is now born," said one man who was called a wise man because he knew many things. "I am going to go and find the king."

"So am I, so am I," said other wise men.

The wise men decided to take gifts for the new king.

They took gold. It sparkled like bits of sunshine.

They took a jar of frankincense. It smelled like flowers.

They took a box of myrrh. It smelled like spices.

The wise men got on their camels and started on their long trip.

They rode over mountains,
they rode through valleys,
they rode through deserts, they rode through forests. At last they came to the big city of Jerusalem.

"Can you tell us where the new king is?" they asked a man in Jerusalem. "We have seen His star and have come to pray to Him."

"A new king!" the man said. "No, I have never heard of Him."

"A new king!" said another man. "Of course not. We have a king. We do not need another king."

"Ask King Herod," said a third man. "Maybe he knows

something about it and can tell you where to go."

When King Herod heard the wise men's question, he was worried. He did not want anyone else to become king. But he found out that long ago a prophet had said the new king was to be born in Bethlehem. The new king was the baby Jesus.

113

King Herod told the wise men to look for the baby Jesus in Bethlehem. "When you have found Him, come and tell me, so I can go and pray to Him, too," he said.

So the wise men got on their camels again. They wondered how they would find Jesus.

Suddenly one wise man called, "Look, look! The star!"

There was the star they had seen at home!

The wise men followed the star until it shone above a little house in Bethlehem.

They got off their camels. They took their gifts and carefully carried them to the door. One wise man knocked.

Knock, knock, knock!

They waited. Was this really the right place?

Then they heard someone coming, and the door opened. They went in and there was Mary with baby Jesus. He stretched His hands out to them!

The wise men knelt down before Jesus and prayed to Him.

Then one wise man gave baby Jesus gold, sparkling like bits of sunshine.

Another wise man gave baby Jesus frankincense, sweet as the smell of flowers.

And another wise man gave baby Jesus myrrh, strong with the smell of good spices.

Then the wise men went home again. They did not stop in Jerusalem, though, because God told them not to tell Herod where the baby Jesus was. The wise men went back to their country on a different road.

# THE TRIP TO EGYPT

Matthew 2:13-23

When King Herod found out that the wise men went home without telling him where he could find the baby Jesus, he was very angry.

Herod did not want to pray to Jesus as he had told the wise men. He wanted to kill Him.

God quickly sent an angel to Joseph.

"Joseph, Joseph!" said the angel to Joseph in a dream. "Get up! Take the baby Jesus and His mother far away to the land of Egypt and stay there until I tell you. King Herod wants to kill the baby."

115

Joseph got up right away. He woke Mary.

"Mary," he said, "King Herod wants to kill the baby Jesus. We have to take Him to Egypt right away."

Mary got up quickly.

She put the baby's things and some clothes for herself and Joseph into a bundle. She packed some food.

Then Mary picked up the baby very gently so He would not wake up, and put a blanket around Him.

Joseph got the donkey ready for the trip. He fastened the bundle on its back. He helped Mary to get on the donkey, and then he put the baby Jesus in her arms.

Joseph led the donkey along the quiet streets of Bethlehem.

It was still dark night,

and nobody saw them go.

The little hooves of the donkey made hardly a sound. Joseph and Mary were quiet so no one would hear them, and the little baby Jesus was fast asleep. On and on they went--

up and down the hills,

across the dry land,

and past the waving palm trees.

Finally they came to the wide blue River Nile in the land of Egypt.

"Now we are safe," said Joseph. "We shall find a little place to live, and stay here until God tells us that we can go back to our own country."

And that is what they did. Mary and Joseph and little Jesus lived in Egypt until one night Joseph heard God's angel calling him again.

"Joseph, Joseph," said the angel, "take Jesus and His mother and go home now. King Herod is dead."

How happy Mary and Joseph were as they packed their things!

They did not have to be quiet.

They did not have to go at night.

And they did not have to hide.

"Good-bye!" they called to their friends and neighbors.

"Good-bye! We are going home."

# IN HIS FATHER'S HOUSE

Luke 2:41-51

Every year Mary and Joseph went from Nazareth to the temple in Jerusalem to celebrate the Passover. The Passover was a very special feast.

Mary and Joseph told Jesus about the beautiful temple. They told Him that people from all over the land came to the temple to pray to God. Jesus could hardly wait till He could see it.

When Jesus was twelve years old, Mary and Joseph said, "Jesus, this year You may come with us to Jerusalem. This year You will be in the temple for the Passover."

Jesus was excited. He ran to tell His friends. "I am going to Jerusalem for the Passover!" He called.

"We are going, too!" said some of the other boys. They made plans to walk together because the trip would take four or five days.

Early one morning, when it was still dark, Mary came to Jesus' bed and said, "Jesus, get up! It is time to go to Jerusalem."

Jesus was wide awake in a minute and jumped up.

Soon they were on their way. It seemed strange to walk past the houses so early in the morning before the sun was up.

It seemed strange to see the dark trees against the sky.

It seemed strange to hear their neighbors walking with them in the dark.

They walked,
and walked,
and walked.

The birds were singing, and then finally the sun rose and it was light.

Jesus and His friends wondered what the temple would be like and who would see it first. But they knew they had to walk several days and sleep several nights before they would come to Jerusalem.

At last one day, they saw the houses of Jerusalem far away up on a hill. And high above them all, they saw the great white temple! They were all so happy that they started singing.

119

They sang, "How lovely is thy dwelling place, O Lord of hosts! . . . My heart and flesh sing for joy to the living God."

Jesus and Mary and Joseph walked up the hill. They walked up the steps to the temple. They walked through the big gates.

Jesus looked all around. He saw the soft curtains and touched them. He smelled the sweet perfume. He heard beautiful singing and playing of instruments. He bowed His head and prayed.

Mary and Joseph and all the other people prayed, too. They all brought their gifts to God.

After the Passover feast was ended, all the people started to go home again. Mary and Joseph left, too. They thought Jesus was walking with the other boys the way He had done before. But when they stopped for the night, Jesus was not there.

Mary and Joseph asked their friends, "Have you seen Jesus?"

"No," said their friends. "We have not seen Him."

Mary and Joseph looked everywhere. They called, "Jesus, where are You?" But there was no answer.

Mary and Joseph were worried. They went back to Jerusalem. They went into the temple. And there at last they found Jesus. He was talking with the teachers.

Mary and Joseph were surprised.

"Son," said His mother. "Why did You do this? Your father and I have been looking for You!"

Jesus looked up. "But why were you looking for Me?" He said. "Do you not know that I belong here? Do you not know that I must be in My Father's house?"

Jesus knew that the temple belonged to God, and that God was His Father.

Then Jesus went home with Mary and Joseph. He loved and obeyed them.

# JESUS COMES HOME

Luke 4:16-30

When Jesus had grown to be a man, He worked hard in a carpenter shop in Nazareth to make a living. But one day He left home to tell people all over the country about God. His mother and sisters and brothers stayed in Nazareth.

After a while Jesus came back to Nazareth to visit.

121

On the Sabbath day He went to the synagogue to pray to God, the way He always did.

His friends and neighbors were glad to see Him in the synagogue. They said, "Please read the Bible to us today."

Jesus stood up. He opened the Bible and read, "God is with me, because he has chosen me to tell good news to those who are poor.

"God has sent me to tell the people who are in prison that they can be free.

"He has sent me to tell those who are blind that they will be able to see.

"He has sent me to help those who are not treated fairly, and to tell all people that God loves them."

Then Jesus closed the book and sat down. Everyone in the synagogue looked at Him.

"I am the One the Bible tells about," Jesus said to them. "God has sent Me."

At first the people liked what Jesus said, but they were surprised. "Jesus is our neighbor," they said. "He is a man just like everyone of us. How does He know that God has sent Him?"

Then the people became very angry. They stopped listening to Jesus and put Him out of the city. They tried to throw Him off a steep hill, but Jesus left them and walked sadly away. He wanted to help the people in His hometown, but they would not let Him.

# A VISIT WITH JESUS

John 1:32-42

When Jesus was on earth, there lived a man called John the Baptist. God sent John to tell the people about Jesus.

"Jesus is the Son of God," said John.

One day John and two of his friends were talking together.

"I wish we could meet Jesus," said one of the friends named Andrew. "Do you know where He is staying?"

"Sh--" said John. "There He is!"

The two friends turned around quickly. They saw Jesus walking down the road.

"Come on," said Andrew to his friend. "Let's go and talk to Him."

Andrew and his friend hurried after Jesus, but they

123

did not know whether they should call Him or not. After all, they had not seen Jesus before.

Suddenly Jesus stopped and turned around. "Are you looking for something?" He asked.

"Teacher," said Andrew, "we were just wondering-- where are You staying?"

"Come with Me and see," said Jesus. "I am going there now. Will you visit Me for a little while?"

That is just what Andrew and his friend hoped Jesus would say, and so they went with Him.

They had a wonderful time. Jesus listened to them. He answered their questions. He told them about God. Then Jesus asked them about their families.

"I have a brother called Simon," said Andrew. "I wish he could talk with You, Jesus!"

"Why don't you bring him?" said Jesus. "I would like to see him."

Andrew hurried home. "Simon, Simon!" he called. "We have found the Messiah."

"The Messiah!" said Simon.

"Yes, His name is Jesus. I am sure He is the One God promised to send. He is the Son of God. And He is right here in our own town!" said Andrew all excited. "Come quickly. He wants to see you."

Simon jumped up. He went with Andrew to Jesus' house.

Jesus looked at Simon. Then He said, "So you are Simon. Someday you will be a good, strong man, Simon. I am going to call you Simon Peter, strong as rock!"

Simon loved Jesus right away. Andrew could see that. He was glad he had brought his brother to see Jesus.

# GOD TAKES CARE OF US

Matthew 5:1,2; 6:25-33

Jesus chose twelve men to be His disciples. They were with Him to learn from Him.

One day Jesus and His disciples were walking along the road. Pat--pat--pat, went their feet on the hard ground. They had walked a long way. They were hungry and tired.

"What are we going to eat today?" asked one of Jesus' disciples. "I am hungry."

"We have some fish," said a disciple who was carrying the lunch. "We have a piece of bread for each one of us and some fruit."

"Well, I guess that is enough for today, but what about tomorrow?" asked another disciple. "There will be no food left."

The disciples looked worried. Would they have nothing to eat tomorrow? They looked at Jesus.

But Jesus did not say anything. They knew Jesus heard them, but He just kept on walking.

Later they went up a mountain. There Jesus sat down. His disciples sat down around Him on the grass.

A little bird came, too. It hopped closer and closer to Jesus.

Hop,
    hop,
        hop.
It cocked its little head and looked at Jesus. Then it picked up some seeds from the ground for its dinner.

Peck,
    peck,
        peck.
Jesus smiled. Then He looked at His disciples. "See

125

this little bird?" He asked. "Who is giving it food to eat?"

The disciples looked surprised. They knew the little bird was picking up seeds that had fallen from the bushes.

Jesus smiled again. He said, "God, our heavenly Father, planned for little birds to get food outdoors. He cares for them. But He cares even more for you.

"I heard you ask if we would have food tomorrow. Do not worry about that. God knows that you need food, and He will take care of you."

126

# JESUS HEALS A LITTLE BOY

John 4:46-54

In the town of Capernaum there lived a father and mother and a little boy.

Every day when Father came home from work, the boy ran out to meet him. "Daddy, Daddy!" he shouted. Father swung his son high up on his shoulders and then they both ducked to get through the door.

One day when Father came home, the little boy did not run to meet him.

"Where is my boy?" thought Father.

Father went into the house. Mother came out of one of the rooms and said, "Our boy is very, very sick."

Quickly Father went into his son's room. "Daddy, my head hurts. I'm hot," said the little boy.

Father and Mother tried everything they could think of to make their boy well again, but nothing helped. What should they do!

Just then a servant, who helped Father and Mother in the house, said to Father, "Sir, I have just heard that Jesus has come to Cana."

"Jesus!" cried Father. "He will help us. Quick, bring me my coat. I will run and get Jesus before our boy dies."

Father told Mother where he was going and rushed out of the house and down the street. He went to Cana as fast as he could go.

"Where is Jesus?" he asked a man he met on the street.

"Over there," said the man and pointed to a crowd of people in an open place between the houses. "The people all want to see Jesus do strange and wonderful things."

Father hurried over to the crowd. He pushed his way

127

through until he stood before Jesus.

"Jesus," said Father, all out of breath, "please come to my house right away. My little boy is very sick. Please come and make him well again."

Jesus looked sad. "Everyone wants to see Me do strange and wonderful things," He said. "Is that what you want, too?"

"Oh, no, no!" said Father. "I want my son to be well again. He is dying. Please come!"

Jesus looked into Father's eyes. Then He put His hand on Father's shoulder and said, "I am sorry your little boy is ill. Go home now. Your son will live."

Father believed what Jesus said. He hurried home. He could hardly wait until he could see his little boy healthy and well again.

Suddenly he saw several of his servants running to meet him.

"Sir," they called, "your son is alive--he is well again."

Father's eyes shone. "When did he get well?" he asked. The men told him.

"That is exactly when Jesus said to me, 'Go home now, your son will live,'" said Father.

They hurried on. When they came near the house, Father saw Mother and his little boy standing in the door.

"Daddy, Daddy!" called the little boy and ran to meet him.

Father swung his boy high up on his shoulders and let him ride into the house.

"Thank you, God, that our boy is well again," said Father. "Thank you for Jesus. Now we know that You sent Him to help us."

# JESUS FORGIVES SIN

Matthew 9:2-8; Mark 2:2-12; Luke 5:18-26

A sick man lay on a mat in a small, dark room. He was all alone. It was hot. The sick man could not move his arms or his fingers. When he wanted a drink, he could not get one.

Far, far away he could hear a noise. He listened. It sounded as if many people were walking and talking. And then everything was quiet again. He wondered what was going on, but he could not get up to look.

Then he heard someone running. Klick-klick-klack. The steps were coming closer. The next minute someone came through the door. It was his friend.

"Jesus is back in town," said his friend. "We will take you to Him. He can make you well."

The sick man groaned. "No, oh, no!" he said. "Jesus will know that I have been a bad man. Surely He will not want to make me well."

"Listen," said the sick man's friend, "we have no time to talk now. Jesus will help you just as you are."

Three other men came in to help. Each took one corner of the mat on which the sick man was lying. Quickly they went down the street to the house where Jesus was.

When they came to the door, they saw they could not get in. People were crowded around the door. People filled the whole house.

They were standing on tiptoe to see Jesus. They were listening to what Jesus was saying.

"Now what will we do?" asked one of the friends.

"We should never have come," groaned the sick man.

"But we have come," said his friend, "and we will

130

find a way to get to Jesus."

And they did.

The four men carried their sick friend up the outside steps to the flat roof of the house. Then they took some tiles out of the roof. They lowered the mat with their friend

131

on it through the hole into the room below. Down he came, right in front of Jesus!

Jesus stopped speaking. He looked at the sick man. He saw the four men peering into the room from the hole above.

Jesus smiled. He was glad the four men had brought their friend to Him. Then He said softly to the sick man, "My son, what you did wrong—your sins—are all forgiven. Do not worry about them anymore!"

The sick man just looked and looked into Jesus' face, he was so happy.

But some of the people in the room were angry. "Who can forgive sins but God?" they thought.

Jesus knew what they were thinking. He said, "I am able to forgive sins. I will show you that this is true." Then Jesus turned to the sick man and said, "Stand up, take your mat, and go home."

The sick man, who had not been able to move at all before, got up. The people were surprised.

Then the man picked up his mat. The people stared at him.

The man started walking. The people got out of the way. They had never seen anything like this happen before. They watched the man hurrying down the street to his house, singing praises to God.

The people, too, started praising God. "Thank you, God, for sending Jesus," they said. "Thank you that Jesus forgives sins and makes sick people well."

The four men who brought their sick friend to Jesus, came pounding down from the roof and ran down the street after their friend. They could hardly catch up with him.

# JESUS STILLS A STORM

Matthew 8:23-27; Mark 4:35-41; Luke 8:22-25

One day Jesus got into a boat with His disciples. He said, "Let us go across to the other side of the lake."

The disciples started rowing. Jesus lay down on a cushion in the back of the boat and fell asleep.

Suddenly a great storm came howling--whooo-oo-OOO across the lake. It tossed the little boat up and down,

133

up and down, on the big foamy waves.

The disciples worked hard to keep the boat from sinking.

"How can Jesus sleep through all this?" cried one of the disciples as he pushed his oar into the stormy water.

Just then a huge wave came toward them and went wham, crash, boom, right into the boat. The disciples just let the water run down their faces as they all pulled on the oars as hard as they could.

Jesus was still asleep.

"We--can't--make--it--to--land!" shouted one of the disciples through the storm.

"We'd better wake Jesus," shouted back another disciple.

"Yes, yes, wake Him," shouted the others. The wind was so loud they could hardly hear each other.

Several disciples stumbled over to where Jesus lay. They shook Him and called, "Jesus, help us! We are sinking. Don't You care at all?"

Jesus sat up and looked calmly into the storm. "Why are you afraid?" He said to His disciples. "Am I not with you?"

Then Jesus stood up and stretched His hand out over the stormy waters. "Be still!" He said.

Immediately the wind stopped blowing. The waves became quiet and gently splashed, shhh-shhh-shhh, against the boat. The storm was over.

The disciples rowed the boat to land. "How is this possible?" they kept thinking. "The wind and the waves do not listen to us! What kind of man is Jesus that even the wind and the water obey Him?"

# JESUS GIVES LIFE

Mark 5:22-24, 35-43

Jairus hurried along the road. He was very sad. He had only one daughter and she was sick. Jairus was looking for Jesus. He wanted Jesus to make his girl well again.

At last Jairus found Jesus. He was standing in the middle of a crowd of people. Jairus quickly pushed through the crowd. He cried, "My little daughter is dying, Jesus. Come and put Your hand on her so that she will be well again."

135

Jesus stopped talking, and went home with Jairus. But before they came to Jairus' house, some people met them and said to Jairus, "Your little girl is dead. Do not bother Jesus anymore. It is too late."

Jairus sat down on a stone and put his head in his hands. He had tried so hard to find Jesus, and now it was too late!

But suddenly he felt Jesus' hand on his shoulder, and he heard Jesus saying, "Jairus, do not be afraid. It is not too late. Just believe that I will help you."

Jairus jumped up and looked into Jesus' face. Quickly he took Jesus to his house. There were many people there. They were crying because the little girl was dead, but Jesus said to them, "Why are you crying? The child is not dead. She is sleeping."

Then Jesus sent all the people away and let Jairus and his wife take Him into the room where the little girl was lying on her bed.

Jesus took the little girl's hand in His strong, warm hand and said, "Little girl, get up!"

The little girl, who had been dead, opened her eyes as if she had just been sleeping. She got up. She walked! Her father and mother could hardly believe their eyes. They took their little girl in their arms and held her close.

Jesus watched them, His eyes shining with happiness. He was glad for Jairus and his wife because their little daughter was alive again.

"Don't forget to give her something to eat," Jesus told them. "She needs food to grow strong and healthy again."

# JESUS GIVES FOOD

John 6:5-14; Matthew 14:14-21; Mark 6:34-44; Luke 9:11-17

All day long Jesus had been talking to a big crowd of people and healing those who were sick.

It was late in the day, but the people were not going home.

Jesus' disciples were worried. "When are these people going home?" they asked each other. "We have nothing here to eat."

One of the disciples whispered to Jesus, "Why don't You send the people away? They need to get something to eat."

Jesus looked up.

137

"You are right," He said. "It is time to eat. But let's not send them away. They are tired. Why don't you give them something to eat?"

"Give them something to eat?" the disciples asked, surprised. "Why, we have no food here!"

"Really?" said Jesus. "None at all?"

"There is a boy here who has some food," said the disciple Andrew. "Let's see--he has one, two, three, four, five rolls; and he has two little fish. But, of course, that is not nearly enough for so many people."

"Oh, we will see," said Jesus. "Bring me the rolls and the fish and ask the people to sit down on the grass."

The disciples did not know what Jesus would do, but they asked the people to sit down as Jesus said. There were about five thousand men besides women and children.

After the people were seated, Jesus took the rolls and the fish in His hands and said, "Thank you, God, for this food. Thank you for the boy who brought it."

Then Jesus handed out the rolls and fish to His disciples, and they gave the food to the people. Everyone had as much as he wanted. There was enough food for everyone.

When the people had eaten, Jesus said to His disciples, "Now gather up the leftovers. We do not want to waste food."

The disciples gathered up the crumbs and scraps, and to their surprise, they got twelve baskets full. Much, much more was left over than they had had to begin with.

Where did the food come from? The people knew Jesus had made it become more. They said, "Jesus can do wonderful things! He must have come from God."

# THANK YOU, JESUS

Luke 17:11-19

One day when Jesus and His disciples were walking along the road, they suddenly heard someone calling, "Jesus, please, please, help us!"

Jesus looked up. He saw ten men standing a little ways off, looking at Him.

The men did not come closer. They just stood there and stretched out their hands to Jesus.

139

The men had sores on their hands.

They had sores on their feet.

They had sores all over.

They had a sickness called leprosy.

Jesus knew that no one wanted to get close to these men.

No one wanted to touch them.

No one wanted to eat with them.

Everyone was afraid he might get the sickness from them. The sick men had to stay way out in the fields, and could not go home. Jesus knew that they were very unhappy.

"Go and show yourself to the priests," said Jesus. "The priests will see that you are well again and give you permission to go home."

At first the men just looked at Jesus. They were so surprised.

Then one man turned and started hobbling toward the priest's house. His feet were still sore. But Jesus had said they would be healed, and he believed Jesus.

Another man turned around, too.

Soon one, two, three, four, five men were on their way. And then six, seven, eight, nine, ten men were all going to the priest's house.

As they went, they saw their sores were gone. They were not crippled anymore. They could run! They shouted for joy.

Jesus and His disciples watched them go. Suddenly one man stopped.

He turned around.

He came running back.

He was laughing, and he kept saying,

"God is good, God is good. Oh, God is good! He sent us Jesus."

Then the man knelt down before Jesus and said, "Thank you! Thank you for making me well so I can go home again!"

The man was from the country of Samaria.

Jesus looked around. He said, "Did I not heal ten men? Where are the other nine? Did no one come back to thank God except this man from another country?"

Then Jesus smiled at the man kneeling before Him. "Get up," He said to him. "I am glad you can go home. You have become well because you believed that I could help you."

# A GOOD NEIGHBOR

Luke 10:25-37

Jesus told many stories. One day He told this one:

A man was walking from the city of Jerusalem to the city of Jericho. He was all alone. No one else was on the road, and on both sides of the road there were big rocks.

The man was afraid that robbers might be hiding behind the rocks. Pat, pat, pat, went his sandals along the road. Thump, thump, thump, went his heart inside. If he could only reach the city of Jericho before too long.

And then it happened. Robbers jumped from behind the rocks. They beat the man. They took his clothes. They took his money. Then they ran away, and left the man to die.

The poor man lay on the hard rocks in the hot sun. The robbers had hurt him so much that he could not get up.

He had nothing to eat.

He had nothing to drink.

And he hurt all over.

Would no one come to help him? He listened.

After a while, he heard someone coming, pat, pat, pat, down the road. Oh, how glad the man was!

But the pat, pat, pat, went right past him. He could not turn his head, but out of the corners of his eyes he saw that the man walking by him was a priest.

The sick man groaned. The priest had seen him, but did not stop to help him. The priest walked by on the other side of the road.

Everything was quiet again. The poor man listened. Would no one come to help him?

Again he heard something. Pat, pat, pat, someone else was walking down the road.

But again the pat, pat, pat, went right past him. The sick man saw that the man hurrying by on the other side of the road was a Levite, another worker in the church. The Levite, too, had seen him, but did not help him.

The sick man groaned. He closed his eyes. He did not listen anymore. He hurt too much.

But someone else was coming. Clippety-clop, clippety-clop, a donkey came trotting around the bend in the road. On its back sat a man from the country of Samaria.

The Samaritan saw the man lying beside the road.

"Whoa, donkey, whoa," he said. The donkey stopped. The Samaritan got off and went to the hurt man.

"Oh, my poor man," he said, "I see somebody has beaten you very badly."

Quickly the man from Samaria took some medicine out of his bag. He cleaned the man's wounds and bandaged them.

Then he helped the man get on his donkey. He held him so he would not fall off, and then the donkey went slowly down the road--clip-clop, clip-clop.

Finally, they came to a little inn or hotel on the side of the road where they could stay for the night.

The Samaritan put the man to bed and took care of him all night.

The next morning he said to the hotel man, "I have to go now, but here is some money. Please take care of the man until he is well. If you have to spend more, I will pay you when I come back."

The hurt man, lying on his bed, felt much better. He smiled. He was thinking about the man from another country who had been so kind to him.

"That man was a good neighbor to me," he whispered to himself. "I wish all people would be like that."

# THE CHILDREN VISIT JESUS

Mark 10:13-16

"We are going to see Jesus, we are going to see Jesus," sang a little girl as she went hippety-hop across the yard in her clean dress.

"We are going, too," said a little boy who was sitting on the steps of the next house. His face was washed, and he was ready to go.

Soon many, many children and their mothers and fathers were on their way to talk with Jesus.

Some boys and girls ran ahead. Then they raced back. "We saw Jesus," they shouted. "He is over there with all the people."

"Sh-sh," said their mothers. "Don't be so loud."

The children walked quietly as they came closer.

Jesus' disciples saw them coming. They looked cross.

"What is the meaning of this?" they asked the mothers and fathers. "Why are you bringing these children?"

"We would like our children to learn to know Jesus," said one father. "We brought them so Jesus would pray with them and bless them."

"Well, Jesus doesn't have time right now," said the disciples. "You can see He is busy."

The boys and girls hid behind their mothers and fathers.

Then Jesus saw what His disciples were doing. "You are not sending the children away, are you?" He said. "No, no! Let the children come to me. Do not stop them, for to such belongs the kingdom of heaven."

Jesus held out His arms, and the children ran to Him.

Jesus sat down, and talked with each little boy and girl. He put His hands on their heads and blessed them.

Then the children went home with their mothers and fathers.

"Good-bye, Jesus! Good-bye, Jesus!" they called.

"Good-bye," Jesus called back.

The little boys and girls went running, hoppety-skip, down the road. They were glad that Jesus was their friend.

# MARY AND MARTHA

Luke 10:38-42

Once there were two sisters. Their names were Mary and Martha. They had a brother whose name was Lazarus. The three of them knew Jesus and loved Him.

One day Lazarus came into the house and called, "Martha! Where are you? Mary! Jesus is coming down the road."

"You don't say!" cried Martha, all excited. "Well! Don't stand there. Go meet Him and tell Him to come here for dinner."

Lazarus hurried out.

"Mary, help me," said Martha as she ran to the back of the house. "We will have to start cooking dinner before Jesus gets here."

Mary looked sad. She went to Martha who was getting out pots and pans. Mary said softly, "Martha, Jesus does not come very often. We have so little time to talk with Him, let's not spend all our time cooking a meal. Let's just eat what we have ready."

But Martha did not hear what Mary said. She was too busy deciding what to make. When Lazarus brought Jesus into the house, Mary and Martha welcomed Him.

After Jesus sat down, Martha hurried back to her cooking. But Mary sat and listened to Jesus. She forgot about helping with the meal.

Suddenly Martha came back into the room where Jesus was. She was angry.

"Mary," she cried, "there you sit! Jesus, don't You care at all that Mary has left me to do all the work alone? Tell her to help me!"

Mary looked down.

Jesus looked at Mary and then at Martha. He saw that they both loved Him.

148

"Martha, Martha," said Jesus, "you are very busy and worried about many things, aren't you? I am glad you want to make a good meal for us, but I would much rather you had a little more time to talk with Me. Mary is doing the one thing that is important right now. Please don't spoil it for her."

# JESUS VISITS ZACCHAEUS

Luke 19:1-10

Nobody liked Zacchaeus.

He lived in a big beautiful house, but nobody came to see him.

He had lovely clothes, but nobody invited him to a party.

Zacchaeus had taken money away from many people, and so no one liked him.

Zacchaeus was lonely and sad in his big house. He wanted someone to love him. He wanted someone to talk to him.

One day he heard a man say, "Jesus is on His way to Jerusalem. He will walk through our town today."

Zacchaeus pretended he had not heard what the man said, but he was very excited. Jesus was coming! Zacchaeus had heard that Jesus talked to all people, even to those who had done bad things.

"I wish I could see Jesus," thought Zacchaeus. But how could he? Zacchaeus was very short. He would not be able to see over the heads of the people crowding around Jesus.

Suddenly Zacchaeus had a good idea. He ran to a spot where Jesus would pass by.

Zacchaeus climbed up a tree and waited. He was glad that he would be able to take a good look at Jesus as He walked by, without being seen by Jesus or by anyone else.

Zacchaeus sat very quietly in the tree. Far away he heard a dog barking. Then he heard children running by and laughing. No one noticed Zacchaeus up in the tree.

Zacchaeus waited and waited. Had Jesus taken a

149

different road? Then Zacchaeus heard a big crowd of people talking. The crowd was coming nearer.

Zacchaeus looked through the leaves to see better.

Soon many people were walking underneath the tree. Zacchaeus could see the tops of their heads and part

150

of their faces. He knew them all. They were people who lived in his town.

Then Zacchaeus saw a man whom he did not know. That must be Jesus. Zacchaeus bent forward as far as he could.

But then he bent back quickly, because Jesus had stopped right under the tree. Jesus looked up at Zacchaeus.

"Zacchaeus," said Jesus, smiling, "hurry and come down. I want to come to your house today."

Zacchaeus almost fell out of the tree he was so surprised. Jesus wanted to come to his house! Jesus wanted to talk with him!

Quickly Zacchaeus climbed down. The people looked at Jesus and then at Zacchaeus. They grumbled. They did not like this at all.

"Zacchaeus has taken money away from people. He has cheated," they said. "Jesus should not go to his house."

But Jesus did not care what anybody said. He loved Zacchaeus. And Zacchaeus did not care what they said. He was too happy.

Zacchaeus took Jesus home with him. "Jesus," he said, "I am sorry for the bad things I have done. Now I am going to give half of my things to the poor people. And if I have taken anything away from anyone, I am going to give back four times as much."

Jesus smiled at Zacchaeus. He said, "From now on this will be a happy home, Zacchaeus. I have come to help people like you. I have come to help them to know God."

And then Jesus and Zacchaeus had a good visit.

# JESUS, THE KING

Matthew 21:1-11; Mark 11:1-11

Jesus and His disciples were on their way to the city of Jerusalem.

When they were almost there, Jesus stopped and said to His disciples, "I would like two of you to do something for Me. Who wants to help?"

All wanted to help, so Jesus chose two of them and said, "I want you to go to that town over there."

Jesus pointed to some houses not very far away.

"Where the road goes into the town, you will find a young donkey," He said. "No one has ever been on it. Untie it and bring it to Me."

152

The disciples were surprised. "Why, yes," they said slowly, "but don't You think the man to whom the donkey belongs might not want us to take it?"

Jesus smiled. "If anyone asks, just say I need the donkey, and he will let you have it," He said.

The two disciples walked to the town. And there stood the donkey tied to a post, just as Jesus had said. They untied it.

People standing nearby said, "What are you doing, untying that donkey?"

"Jesus needs it," said the disciples. "We will bring it back later."

"All right," said the people.

The disciples brought the donkey to Jesus. They put their coats on the little donkey's back, and Jesus got on. He spoke gently to the donkey. He petted it.

The little donkey pricked up its ears. It had never had a man riding on its back before, but with Jesus it was not wild.

Jesus started riding along the street into Jerusalem.

"Jesus is coming, Jesus is coming!" shouted the children.

"Jesus is riding into Jerusalem," called one man to another.

"We must welcome Him as we would a king!" shouted others.

The people broke branches off the trees and threw them on the road to make a beautiful green path for Jesus to ride on.

They took off their coats and spread them out on the street so Jesus could ride softly.

"Hurrah! Jesus, our king, is coming!" the people shouted. "Blessed is he who comes in the name of the Lord. Hosanna! Hosanna!"

All the people were shouting for joy. They were running ahead of Jesus and following after Him.

"Why all this noise?" asked the people in Jerusalem. "Who is this man riding into Jerusalem like a king?"

"It is Jesus," shouted the people.

"It is Jesus, who helped us when we were sick!"

"It is Jesus, who helped us when we were sad!"

154

"It is Jesus, who has come from God!"

"Thank you, God, for sending us Jesus. Thank you!"

With the people all around Him, Jesus rode into Jerusalem.

# A GIFT FOR JESUS

Matthew 26:1-13

Some people hated Jesus because He told them that they were not obeying God. They hated Him so much that they planned to kill Him.

But there was a woman who loved Jesus. "What can I give Jesus to show Him that I love Him?" she thought.

She went into her room and took a box from a shelf. There were many beautiful things in the box.

She took out some pretty stones. No, they were not the right gift. She took out lovely soft cloth. No, that was not the right gift either.

155

Then she took out a little alabaster jar filled with perfume. The jar felt smooth in her hands. It shone in the sunlight. The perfume smelled like many, many flowers.

The woman held the little jar in her hands. It was the most beautiful thing she had. "I will give this to Jesus," she whispered to herself. "When He smells this perfume, He will know that I love Him."

The woman walked down the street to the house where Jesus and His disciples were eating supper. She tiptoed to the door and looked in. There were many men with Jesus. The woman was afraid to go in.

But then Jesus looked up. He smiled at her, as if to say, "Won't you come in?"

The woman forgot about everyone else in the room. Quickly she walked to Jesus. She opened the lovely little jar and poured the perfume on Jesus' head. The whole room was filled with the beautiful scent.

The disciples were upset. They knew the perfume cost a lot of money. "Why did you do such a silly thing?" they asked the woman. "Why, if you had sold that perfume, you could have given much money to the poor."

The woman was frightened. Had she done the wrong thing? She looked at Jesus. Was He angry with her, too?

No, Jesus was not angry. He understood her. He turned to His disciples and said, "Leave her alone! This woman has given me the most beautiful thing she had. Do you know why? Because I will die soon. People will always remember what she has done for Me."

The woman walked slowly down the street to her home. "Jesus liked my gift," she thought. "Jesus understood that I love Him."

# JESUS DIES

John 14–19; Matthew 26, 27; Luke 22, 23

Two days after the woman gave Jesus her gift, Jesus had a special supper with His disciples.

"This is the last time we shall eat together before I die," Jesus said.

The disciples were very sad. They did not want Jesus to die.

157

"For a little while you won't be able to see Me," said Jesus, "but then I will come back again. So don't be sad. You will see Me again."

After that Jesus prayed. They sang together. Then Jesus and His disciples went to a garden not far from Jerusalem.

Jesus went to the garden to pray. Jesus told the disciples to pray, too.

It was late in the evening and the disciples were sleepy. They sat down and soon fell asleep.

But Jesus prayed. He knew He would soon die. He wanted to talk about this with God.

Suddenly there was much noise in the garden.

A group of people along with soldiers carrying weapons and lights came up the garden path. They were looking for Jesus. They wanted to arrest Him and put Him to death even though Jesus had done nothing wrong.

Jesus came forward.

"For whom are you looking?" Jesus asked.

"For Jesus," they said.

"I am He," Jesus answered.

The soldiers were so surprised that they stepped back and fell to the ground.

Jesus asked them again, "For whom are you looking?"

"For Jesus," they said again.

"I told you I am He," said Jesus. "If you are looking for Me, take Me, and let My disciples go."

The disciple called Peter jumped up. He did not want the soldiers and the other people to take Jesus away. Quickly he took his sword and swung it at one of the men. He cut off the man's ear!

"No, no, Peter," said Jesus. "Put your sword away.

If I wished, I could ask My heavenly Father for thousands and thousands of angels, and He would send them at once. But I am ready to die as My Father wants Me to."

Then Jesus touched the man's ear and healed him.

It was the last kind thing Jesus could do with His hands, for then the soldiers grabbed Him. They tied His hands and took Jesus away.

Later the people who did not love Jesus killed Him by nailing Him to a cross. But Jesus loved them and asked God to forgive them.

After Jesus died, His friends buried Him. They were very, very sad.

They were so sad that they forgot that Jesus had told them when they ate supper together, "For a little while you won't be able to see Me, but then I will come back again, and you will see Me."

Of course Jesus would come back! He promised, and Jesus always keeps His promise.

159

# JESUS IS ALIVE!

Matthew 28:1-10

On the third day after Jesus died on the cross, early before the sun was up, Mary Magdalene and Mary were walking sadly along the road.

A little bird started singing, but Mary Magdalene and Mary did not listen.

A pink cloud floated in the sky, but Mary Magdalene and Mary did not look at it.

They were very, very sad. They were going to visit Jesus' grave. They thought they would never, never see Jesus again.

But as they were coming close to the grave something very strange happened. There was a big noise.

The earth began to shake.

The trees swayed back and forth.

The little stones on the road rolled this way and that.

"What is it?" asked Mary Magdalene, holding her head. She thought she must be dizzy.

"It is an earthquake!" cried Mary.

At that moment the sun came up and shone into the garden. The birds sang and whistled and called. Everything was bright and beautiful.

Mary Magdalene and Mary looked surprised. How could everything seem so happy when Jesus was dead! Then Mary looked at the grave. She pointed. Mary Magdalene looked, too.

160

Like lightning that does not go out, an angel was in front of the grave. The angel had rolled away the stone that had been in front of the opening, and was sitting on it.

161

Mary Magdalene and Mary could not move, they were
so frightened.

The angel saw them.

"Do not be afraid," he called out to them with a voice full of joy. "I know you are looking for Jesus, who was dead and buried in this grave.

"He is not here anymore. He is alive again. He has come out of the grave. Come and see! The grave is empty."

Mary Magdalene and Mary could see there was no one in the grave.

"Go quickly and tell His disciples that Jesus has risen from the dead, and that they will see Him," said the angel.

Mary Magdalene and Mary turned around and ran out of the garden. They hardly knew what they were doing, they were so excited and happy.

And suddenly Jesus was standing in front of them.

"Good morning, Mary Magdalene! Good morning, Mary!" He said.

Mary Magdalene and Mary knelt down before Jesus and worshiped Him.

"Do not be afraid," said Jesus to them. "Go and tell the others who love Me that you have seen Me and that they will see Me, too."

Mary Magdalene and Mary got up and ran till they found Jesus' friends and disciples.

"Jesus is alive!" they called. "We have seen Him. He talked to us. Don't be sad anymore. Jesus has come back again!"

That was the first Easter Day. And every Easter since then, people who love Jesus are very, very happy because they remember in a special way that Jesus is alive.

# JESUS GOES TO HEAVEN

John 16:28; Acts 1:1-12

The time had come for Jesus to go back to His heavenly Father. For the last time He walked along the road with His disciples.

For the last time His disciples saw Him.

"Now, remember," Jesus said to His disciples, "I want you to stay in Jerusalem and wait there until the Holy Spirit comes. God promised to send Him."

163

The disciples were excited. "Are You going to be a great king in this country then?" they asked.

"Oh, My friends," said Jesus, "that is something you cannot know. God knows. The important thing is that you tell all people in the world that you have seen Me and known Me. The Holy Spirit will help you."

After Jesus said this, He was lifted up and a cloud came and took Him out of their sight.

The disciples stood and looked and looked up into the blue sky. They could not believe that Jesus was really gone.

But then suddenly two men in white clothes stood beside them.

"Why do you stand here looking into heaven?" they asked. "Jesus has gone to heaven, but someday He will come back just as you saw Him go."

Slowly Jesus' disciples turned away and went down the hill back to Jerusalem.

They were sad that they could not see Jesus anymore, but they were excited that Jesus wanted them to tell all people about Him.

They were glad that the Holy Spirit would help them. They were glad that Jesus would come back someday.

# THE HOLY SPIRIT COMES

Acts 2:1-42

After Jesus had gone to heaven, His disciples stayed in the city of Jerusalem. They remembered that Jesus had told them to wait there until His Spirit would come to them.

They waited and prayed.

"What do you think it will be like when the Holy Spirit comes?" asked one disciple.

"I don't know. I only wish He would come soon," said another disciple. "We have waited so long."

Suddenly one disciple bent forward. "Sh-sh," he said. "What's that?"

The other disciples all listened.

Then they heard it, too. A sound like a great wind was coming toward them.

Then the sound was in the house, and on each disciple's head there was something that looked like a little flame.

Suddenly the disciples knew! God had sent the Holy Spirit.

Outside a great crowd of people gathered to see what was happening. They heard the sound, too, and wondered what was going on.

The disciples came out of the house and spoke to the people. They told them of the wonderful things God had done.

The people were surprised. They could understand every word the disciples were saying even though they came from different countries and spoke different languages.

"What does this mean?" asked the people.

The disciple Peter said, "This means that Jesus, whom you killed, did not stay dead.

"This means that God Himself made Jesus alive again.

"This means that God has sent His Spirit to stay with us.

"God has kept His promise."

Many, many people were glad that the Holy Spirit had come. Three thousand believed what Peter said and were baptized that day.

They stayed together and thanked God. They loved Jesus. They wanted to be His disciples, too, and be part of His church.

# CORNELIUS

Acts 10

Cornelius was a good man. He and his family loved God, and shared their food and clothing with other people. But Cornelius did not know Jesus.

God wanted Cornelius to know Jesus, so one day when Cornelius was praying as usual, God sent an angel to him.

"Cornelius!" said the angel.

Cornelius was afraid. He had never seen an angel before. "What do you want?" he said.

"Cornelius, God has heard your prayers," said the angel, "and God has seen how you share what you have with others.

"Now send some men to the town of Joppa to get a man called Peter. Peter has something to tell you."

When the angel was gone, Cornelius called some of his servants.

"Go quickly to Joppa," he said to them. "There is a man there called Peter who has something to say to me. Bring Peter here as fast as you can."

The servants left immediately to go to Joppa.

When they were gone, Cornelius got everything ready for Peter.

He called his friends.

He called his brothers and sisters.

He called his aunts and uncles.

He called his cousins.

"Come to my house," he said. "A man called Peter is coming to tell me something God wants me to know."

The friends came.

The brothers and sisters came.

The aunts and uncles and cousins came.

They were all ready and waiting at Cornelius' house when at last they saw Peter coming. They did not know who Peter was. They did not know he was one of Jesus' disciples.

When Peter came into the house, Cornelius knelt down before him.

"No, no," said Peter. "Don't kneel before me. I am a man just like you and not an angel.

"But tell me, why did you send for me? God told me to come here, even though you have come from another country and do not belong to God's people.

"I am wondering what this is all about."

Then Cornelius said to him, "A man with bright clothing stood before me while I was praying, and he told me to send for you because you have something to tell me.

"We are all here now to hear what God wants us to know."

Peter was very much surprised.

He said, "Now I know that God wants all people to know about Jesus. It does not matter to God from which country people come or how they look. God loves everyone."

Then Peter told Cornelius and all the people in his house about Jesus.

He told them how kind Jesus was when He was with them.

He told them how Jesus died, and how God brought Him back to life again.

He told them that Jesus wants to help all the people who do wrong.

While Peter was still speaking, the Holy Spirit came to Cornelius and his friends, just like He had come to Jesus' own disciples.

Cornelius and his friends were very, very happy. They could not see Jesus, but they knew He was with them.

They were baptized. From then on Cornelius and his friends were God's people, too, and part of the church.

# PETER AT THE DOOR
Acts 12:1-17

Everywhere Peter went he told people about Jesus. But King Herod did not want Peter to tell people about Jesus. It made him very angry.

"Lock Peter in jail so he can't get out," said King Herod to his soldiers. "When he is in jail, he will not be able to tell people about Jesus."

Herod's soldiers put Peter in jail. They tied his hands with two chains. They watched him all the time so he could not run away.

One night Peter lay down to sleep.

He did not like to sleep in jail.

He did not like to be tied with chains.

He did not like to be watched all the time. But he knew that Jesus was with him even though he could not see Him. And Peter knew that his friends were praying for him.

Suddenly a bright light shone into Peter's little room. God's angel came in. He shook Peter to awaken him.

"Get up quickly," said the angel.

The chains fell off Peter's hands.

"Dress yourself and put on your sandals," said the angel.

Peter dressed himself.

"Put on your coat and follow me," said the angel.

Peter followed the angel.

He did not know whether this was all a dream or whether it was real. But the soldiers who watched Peter did not seem to see what was happening. The angel and Peter walked right by them.

When the angel and Peter came to the big iron gate,

the gate opened in front of them.

    The angel took Peter out into the street a little ways and then left him.

    Peter just stood there in the dark for a little while.

He thought to himself, "Now I am sure that this is real. God sent an angel to bring me out of the jail to save me from King Herod."

Peter quickly walked to the house where he knew his friends were together praying for him.

He knocked at the door. Knock, knock, knock!

A girl called Rhoda came to see who was there.

"Let me in," said Peter.

Rhoda was so glad to hear Peter's voice that she forgot to open the door. She ran back to the others and cried, "It's Peter, it's Peter! He is standing at the door!"

Peter's friends jumped up. "Don't be silly, Rhoda," they said. "Peter is in jail. He can't be here."

"But he is, he is," cried Rhoda. "I heard him."

Knock, knock, knock! Peter kept on knocking. He smiled. He knew his friends just could not believe that he was really there.

Peter's friends came rushing to the door. They looked out.

"Peter!" they cried. "Is it really you?" They pulled Peter in and closed the door. They laughed and cried and talked all at once.

"How did you get out of jail?" they asked.

"God's angel brought me out," said Peter. Then he told them how it all happened.

Peter's friends were glad God heard their prayers. They were glad that Peter was free again.

172

# THE ETHIOPIAN

Acts 8:26-40

Philip was one of Jesus' helpers. He told many people the good news that Jesus loved them.

One day an angel of the Lord said to Philip, "Philip, go and walk along the road that goes from Jerusalem to Gaza."

Philip did not know what God wanted him to do on that road, but he obeyed God and went.

The road was dusty and there were no trees. Philip was all alone on the road as far as he could see.

But suddenly Philip saw a cloud of dust. Someone was coming!

The cloud of dust came nearer and nearer. Then Philip saw that it was a chariot or wagon that was making all that dust.

The chariot was pulled by horses. Clop, clop, clop, went the hooves of the horses.

Philip saw a man who had dark skin sitting in the chariot. He was wearing beautiful clothes. Philip could see that he had come from the faraway country of Ethiopia.

The Holy Spirit said to Philip, "Go and speak to the man in the chariot."

Philip ran up to the chariot. He saw that the man was holding a part of the Bible in his hands, and he could hear him reading out loud.

"Do you understand what you are reading?" Philip asked the Ethiopian.

173

"How can I understand it when no one has ever told me what it means?" said the man from Ethiopia. "Please, come and sit in the chariot with me, so we can talk."

After the chariot stopped, Philip climbed in and sat down beside the man. "God loves us all, and so He sent His Son Jesus to help us," Philip said.

The Ethiopian was very glad to hear about Jesus. He wanted to know more and more about Him. Philip told the man everything he wanted to know.

174    Finally, they came to a place where there was water beside the road.

The Ethiopian said, "Philip, I love Jesus. I want to belong to Him, too, and be a part of His church. Look,

here is some water. Why don't you baptize me?"

Philip was glad that the man from the faraway country of Ethiopia loved Jesus. He and the man got out of the chariot. They went into the water and there Philip baptized the man.

Then the Holy Spirit took Philip away. The man from Ethiopia went on home. He was glad that at last he understood the stories in the Bible, and that he now knew Jesus.

175

# SAUL MEETS JESUS

Acts 9:1-22

Saul hated Jesus. He hated all the people who loved Jesus. Whenever Saul found any of Jesus' friends, he dragged them off to jail or had them killed.

Saul did not know that Jesus was the Son of God.

One day Saul went far away from home to the city of Damascus to look for people who loved Jesus. He wanted to kill them, too.

But on the way something happened. Suddenly a very bright light flashed around Saul. Saul fell to the ground.

Then he heard a voice saying, "Saul, Saul, why are you killing the people who love Me?"

Saul did not know who was speaking, so he said, "Who are You, Lord?"

And the voice said, "I am Jesus, whom you hate."

It was Jesus! Saul had never met Jesus before. Now that he heard His voice, Saul knew that Jesus was good and that He was the Son of God. From now on Saul wanted to obey Jesus.

So Saul said to Jesus, "What do You want me to do?"

Jesus said, "Go into the city of Damascus. There someone will tell you what to do."

When Jesus was gone, Saul stood up. He looked around. But he could not see anything. He was blind.

The men who were with Saul, took him by the hand and led him to the city of Damascus to the house of a friend.

176

There Saul sat. He was blind. He could not see anything. And now that Saul had met Jesus, he was sorry that he had hurt so many of Jesus' friends.

Saul did not know what to do. He thought and thought. He asked God to help him.

All of a sudden he heard someone coming into the room. Saul raised his head.

Then Saul felt strong hands on his shoulders, and he heard a voice saying, "Brother Saul, I am Ananias. The Lord Jesus, whom you saw on the road coming here, has sent me to help you.

"Jesus wants you to see again. He wants to tell you what you can do for Him."

Then Saul was no longer blind. He could see Ananias standing in front of him. And he knew Jesus was with him even though he could not see Him.

Saul was very, very happy. He was baptized to show that he now belonged to Jesus and was a part of His church.

Ananias and Saul ate together. They talked about what Saul would do from now on.

Saul could hardly wait until he could tell everybody about Jesus and how much he loved Him.

Jesus' friends did not have to be afraid of Saul anymore. Now he was their friend, too.

# BARNABAS

Acts 9:26-28

After Saul had met Jesus and learned to love Him, he wanted to meet Jesus' friends in Jerusalem, but they were afraid of him.

Jesus' friends thought Saul was only pretending to love Jesus. They thought Saul would still try to put them

179

in jail and kill them. So Jesus' friends kept very quiet.

They did not tell Saul where they lived.

They did not tell Saul where they met.

They did not tell Saul anything about the church. Saul did not know what to do.

One day Saul met a man called Barnabas. Barnabas was a kind man, and Saul knew that he loved Jesus.

"Barnabas," said Saul, "don't be afraid of me. Believe me, I love Jesus now and won't ever hurt any of His friends again. You see, when I went to Damascus, Jesus talked to me. Now I know that Jesus is the Son of God."

Barnabas looked at Saul.

"I believe you, Saul," he said. "I believe that you love the Lord Jesus."

"Then won't you take me with you, so I can meet Jesus' other friends?" asked Saul.

"Yes," said Barnabas. "I am on my way to see Jesus' friends now. You may come with me if you wish."

Saul was excited. Would Jesus' friends believe that he loved them and did not want to hurt them anymore?

Click, click, click, went Saul's sandals on the road.

Clack, clack, clack, went Barnabas' sandals beside him.

Now Saul had a friend to walk with him.

Finally Saul and Barnabas came to a house and went in. There were many people in the house. Saul saw how frightened they were when he came in.

"It is Saul!" they whispered. "It is Saul himself."

Barnabas put a hand on Saul's shoulder.

"Yes, it is Saul," said Barnabas. "But Saul no longer hates Jesus. Saul loves Jesus now and wants to be our friend. Won't you forgive him and be his friend, too?"

180

The people looked earnestly at Saul. Then they began to smile. They crowded around Saul and talked with him.

Saul was glad to have so many friends. But most of all, he was glad for his good friend Barnabas.

# A MISSIONARY TRIP

Acts 13, 14

After Saul became a friend of Jesus, people began to call him Paul.

Paul and Barnabas were good friends. They liked to do things together.

They liked to teach people the stories about Abraham and Moses and Saul and David.

They liked to tell the people what they knew about Jesus.

One day the Holy Spirit said to the people in the church, "I would like you to send Paul and Barnabas on a long trip to tell people in faraway towns and cities about Me, too."

The people in the church did as the Spirit told them

to do. They had a special church service for Paul and Barnabas.

"Good-bye, Paul. Good-bye, Barnabas!" they said. "Have a safe trip and tell many, many people how great God is. Tell many, many people about Jesus."

Paul and Barnabas started on their long trip. Sometimes they walked, and sometimes they sailed in a big ship.

One day they came to a city. In that city they met a magician.

"Do you know Jesus?" Paul and Barnabas asked the magician.

"No," said the magician. "Who is He?"

Paul and Barnabas told the magician how Jesus lived

and died

    and rose again.

But the magician would not listen. He did not believe Paul and Barnabas. He did not want anybody else to believe them either.

Paul and Barnabas went to another city. There they met many other people.

"Do you know Jesus?" asked Paul and Barnabas.

"No," said the people. "Who is He?"

Paul and Barnabas told the people the stories about Jesus. They told them how Jesus

    lived

      and died

        and rose again.

The people listened a little bit, but then many did not want to hear any more. They became angry. They even wanted to throw stones at Paul and Barnabas.

So Paul and Barnabas went to another city. There they met a man who could not walk.

This man listened very carefully when Paul and Barnabas told the stories about Jesus. This man believed what Paul and Barnabas said, and the Spirit of Jesus made him well again.

Paul and Barnabas told many other people about Jesus. Some did not listen at all. Some listened a little bit. But many people listened very carefully and believed what Paul and Barnabas said about Jesus.

When Paul and Barnabas came home from their long missionary trip, they told the people in their church, "God has done wonderful things with us. Many people have learned to love and obey the Lord Jesus.

"We are glad you sent us on this trip."

# TIMOTHY

Acts 16:1-6

Once there was a little boy called Timothy. He lived with his mother and father and grandmother in the town of Lystra.

Often Timothy climbed on Grandmother's lap and said, "Grandma, tell me a story."

"Which one?" asked Grandma.

Sometimes Timothy said, "Tell me about Abraham."

Sometimes Timothy said, "Tell me the story about Joseph."

Sometimes he said, "Tell me about the baby Moses," but Timothy never said, "Tell me a story about Jesus," because he had never heard a story about Jesus.

His grandmother had never heard about Jesus, and his father and mother had never heard about Him.

One day when Timothy was a young man, Paul and Barnabas came to the town of Lystra where Timothy lived. Paul told the people the good news about Jesus.

Timothy listened carefully.

He thought about Jesus.

He prayed to Him.

He learned to love Him.

"I wish I could help other people to know Jesus, too," he thought.

One day Paul came back to Lystra.

"Timothy," said Paul, "I am on a long trip to tell people about Jesus. Will you go with me and help me?"

"Oh, yes!" said Timothy, "I would like to help you."

So Timothy went along with Paul, and together they
walked

and walked

and walked

through the towns and through the cities to tell people how Jesus lived and died and rose again.

Paul was glad that he had Timothy to help him.

# LYDIA

Acts 16:11-15

In the city of Philippi there lived a lady called Lydia. **187**
Lydia had a store. She sold beautiful purple cloth
in her store. Every day Lydia was in her store to sell her
cloth to people who came in to buy.

But on one day in the week Lydia was not in her store. On the Sabbath day, Lydia went to a special place to pray.

The people in Philippi who loved God came together under the trees near a river to pray.

Lydia liked this place to pray.

The leaves rustled--shh-shh-shh,

the birds sang,

and the water in the river slipped by quietly, as Lydia and her friends talked about God and prayed.

One Sabbath day something very special happened. As Lydia and some friends were sitting by the river, they saw some men coming down the path. They had never seen these men before. Who could they be?

"I am Paul," said one of the men, "and this is Timothy. We are on a trip through the cities to tell people about Jesus. May we pray with you?"

"Oh, yes," said Lydia. "Please do. You say you tell people about Jesus. Who is He?"

"Jesus is the Son of God," said Paul. "God sent Him to show us what God is like."

Lydia and her friends asked many questions. They wanted to know more about Jesus.

After a while Lydia said, "I knew about God for a long time, but I did not know that He sent His Son Jesus. I want to love Jesus, too."

188 Then Lydia and her family were baptized to show that they were a part of the church of Jesus.

Paul and Timothy stayed in Lydia's house while they were in Philippi. Lydia wanted them to be her guests.

# PAUL WRITES A LETTER
The Book of Philippians

A long time after Paul and Timothy left Philippi, Paul was in jail in a faraway city. People who did not like to hear about Jesus put him there.

Now Paul could not go from place to place to tell people about Jesus.

He could not see his friends,
he could not visit them.

Paul wondered if his friends still remembered him and if they still loved Jesus.

One day something very special happened. There was a knock at the door. Knock, knock, knock!

When the jailkeeper opened the door, a man came in.

"Epaphroditus!" cried Paul. "How are you? This certainly is a wonderful surprise. I am glad you have come to see me!"

Epaphroditus had come all the way from Philippi to help Paul and to bring him a gift from Lydia and the other people who were a part of the church there.

Paul was very happy that the people had not forgotten him,

      he was glad that they loved him,

        he was glad that they had sent him a gift.

When Epaphroditus was ready to go home again, Paul said to Timothy, who had also come to see him, "Let's write a letter to the folks in Philippi and send it back with Epaphroditus."

"Yes," said Timothy, "let's do that."

So Paul wrote a letter to the church in Philippi. He said, "I thank God for you people at Philippi whenever I think of you. You are very dear to me. I pray that you may love each other more and more and obey Jesus."

"I am in jail," wrote Paul, "but I am very happy. I know things will turn out for the best because you are praying and because Jesus is helping me.

"Thank you for sending Epaphroditus, and thank you for your gift. Now I have everything I want. And my God will supply every need of yours."

Epaphroditus took the letter back to Philippi. Lydia and the other people who belonged to the church read it. They were glad Paul had written them a letter.

The letter Paul wrote is in the Bible. We can read it there.

# HEAVEN

John 14:1-3; Revelation 21, 22

The Bible tells us about Jesus and what He said when He was here on earth.

One day before Jesus went back to His heavenly Father, He said, "In My Father's house are many rooms. I am going to get everything ready and then I will come again and take you with Me so you are where I am."

We call the place where Jesus is, heaven.

191

Jesus told us about it. He said, "God Himself will live with His people. He will wipe every tear from their eyes.

No one will cry or be sad anymore.
No one will die,
No one will be sick or be hurt,
and there will be no night there."

Jesus said heaven is very beautiful. It is so beautiful that it is hard to describe.

It is like a city of pure gold,
clear as glass
and sparkling like a diamond.

A river flows from the throne of God right through the middle of the street of the city. The tree of life grows on both sides of the river and it has twelve kinds of fruit on it.

But the most wonderful thing of all is that we will see God. Now we can't see Him, but when we are in heaven we will see His face. He will give us His name, and we will stay close to Him and to Jesus all the time.

We know this because Jesus has told us, and Jesus always keeps His promise.